The Black Swan

Memory,
Midlife, and Migration

ANNE BATTERSON

Anne Batterson

A LISA DREW BOOK

SCRIBNER

NEW YORK   LONDON   TORONTO   SYDNEY   SINGAPORE

A LISA DREW BOOK/SCRIBNER
1230 Avenue of the Americas
New York, NY 10020

SCRIBNER and design are trademarks of
Macmillan Library Reference USA, Inc., used under license
by Simon & Schuster, the publisher of this work.

A LISA DREW BOOK is a trademark of Simon & Schuster, Inc.

Designed by Kyoko Watanabe
Text set in Legacy Serif

Manufactured in the United States of America

1   3   5   7   9   10   8   6   4   2

Library of Congress Cataloging-in-Publication Data

Batterson, Anne.
The black swan: memory, midlife, and migration/Anne Batterson.
p. cm.
"A Lisa Drew Book."
1. Middle age. I. Title.
HQ1059.4 .B37 2001
305.244—dc21   2001018203

ISBN-10: 1-4165-7509-X
ISBN-13: 978-1-4165-7509-2

For David
For my children and their children
and for all the birds

The way we are living,
timorous or bold,
will have been our life.

SEAMUS HEANEY

Contents

Author's Note

While this is a work of nonfiction, I have, at times, altered specific details to protect the privacy of the people I have written about.

During and after my trip I read a good deal about migrating birds. While writing the book I relied on *The Audubon Society Encyclopedia of North American Birds,* edited by John K. Terres, and *The Random House Atlas of Bird Migration,* edited by Jonathan Elphick, for supporting detail and to check the accuracy of my assumptions.

Acknowledgments

The black swan herself would be inside a coyote right now were it not for the instincts, compassion, and dedication of Jay Kaplan, director of Roaring Brook Nature Center, and the vision of Kem Appell of the Connecticut Waterfowl Trust, who gave her sanctuary.

Writing and then publishing a first book is an adventure of the highest order. You begin nowhere and end up beyond your wildest dreams. It is a journey from self-doubt to self-doubt to self-doubt punctuated by moments of the weirdest mania. It is the life of a blowfish. I could never have had the fortitude for this if it were not for the people I met along the way who are passionate about the written word the way other people are passionate about basketball or gardening. I will be forever grateful to June Wassel, who pointed out the way; to my unflappable writers' group who hung in there with me week after month after year—Lou Mandler, Pam Kelly, Caroline Soutter, and Louise Feldman; for the miracles of Bread Loaf Writers' Conference: Scott Russell Sanders, whose insight and support made every difference, and Carol Houck

Smith, who put me under her wing during early drafts; for my Olympian agent Malaga Baldi and her lightning bolts, who beamed me into the hallowed realm of my wondrous editor, Lisa Drew. Who would have dreamt it.

The Black Swan

1

The Restlessness

I am inside the cloud now, flying blind. I scan the drifting shadows for a sign, a flash of earth or sky, something that will tell me where I am. The altimeter mounted on my reserve parachute reads 3,500 feet. I tap the glass a few times to make sure the needle isn't stuck. I look over at the red handle of my rip cord. "Not yet," I tell myself. "Trust your instruments." Just as my fingers fold around the cold metal grip, the ground smashes through the cloud, huge, brown, hard. Panicking, I fight the impulse to pull, knowing that this is the ground-rush effect, not the real thing; knowing too that I will end up landing in the trees if I open my parachute too high.

At 2,200 feet, I give a sharp yank and feel the pins slide out, the snap of my pack as it opens up. Arching back, I watch the small white pilot chute pop free over my head and catch the air. Attached to it, the red-white-and-blue sleeve of my parachute comes snaking out until it stands straight up like a candle. The weight of my falling body pulls the parachute out of the sleeve. It flowers slowly, uncupping delicately against the sky.

Although this particular moment happened more than thirty years ago, it remains, quite simply, the story of my life.

*   *   *

"What the hell are you doing, Anne Batterson?" I whisper as I begin stowing the last batch of groceries into the back of the camper. The question makes me laugh out loud. And then it makes me scared.

What is it that makes me bolt out the door the way I do, take such hefty risks with my second marriage, my teaching job at the university, my delicately balanced relationship with David's parishioners, my own sanity?

The perennial ring of these questions catches me off guard. I stand in the middle of the driveway, a bottle of olive oil in my hand, shaking my head slowly but also grinning. I know it is the September light that makes me do these things, but I just can't go around saying that to people.

I have always known a wild bird lives inside of me. Have felt it gazing quietly through my eyes, tipping my head back to read the slender twists of mares' tails, the mapping of the stars. And too, there are dreams that are not my own. Dreams of homing, of soaring high above the earth, silent as a glider, following the ancient bearings my body knows. When the weather turns in August, the creature frets and frets until it makes me feel edgy, deprived, skewed somehow—by the tilting of the light.

I used to fly airplanes for a living. Other things as well: parachutes, soaring planes, antique biplanes upside down. This helped. In more recent years I have flown off to Nepal most Octobers, to guide treks high up into the mountains where the light blinds the mind. Extreme measures, I know, just for a little light, a little momentum. But of course, there was more propelling these migrations. Rapture, for one thing. Fear, for another. The trick was to keep the cycle moving. The light, the shadow. The light.

Two things my father used to say about me turned out to be true. The first was that I was destined to marry an itinerant trombone player. I did that the first time around. Did I ever. That guy could orchestrate anything, from the story of his life to the music of the spheres.

The second thing my father liked to say was that when I *really* fell in love, I would "go down like a tent." I never knew what that meant until I met David nine years ago, when I was forty-six. It happened the first time I looked into those prismatic blue eyes. Ploof. In fact, I still fold up inside when I see him through the door of his office at home, feet propped up on his desk, phone curled into his shoulder. He always brightens when he sees me, dandles his head as if whoeveritis will never stop talking, so that I cannot resist going to him to touch his shoulders through his cotton shirt and kiss him softly in the hollow of his free temple.

I accepted these events foretold along with the birth of two daughters as strokes of the cycle, like day and night—although at times they felt more like life and death.

But somewhere in the past couple of years, I started losing momentum. This happened gradually—after the last of our parents died, and the children's bedrooms became clean and still except for the gauzy curtains, lifting and falling in the long afternoons like huge silent lungs. David and I began to face off at each other every time we tried to talk about the future. *Retirement,* he would try out over the dinner table, *Montana. Photography. More time. Enough time. Fifteen years if I'm lucky,* he would say with a sigh.

What I heard was: *Hurry. Hurry. There's no time. It's almost over.*

I couldn't do it, that conversation. The language was all wrong, and I had no words to offer. Up until then, I had lived my life as if it were a never-ending series of intriguing chapters, each one more compelling than the last. My eyes were invariably on the one ahead, and the next, so much so that I was absurdly unprepared for the chapter David wanted me to contemplate. Maybe nothing could have prepared me for that singular moment when the rest of my life unfurled before me in one seamless piece, like a winding sheet.

After that, my universe tightened up like a fist, very slowly. So slowly I could not name my losses until they were long gone: the trail that once cut up the ridge behind our house, the exact weight of a child on my hip, calling my mother on the kitchen phone to chat while I washed lettuce and chopped up vegetables for dinner.

The harder David struggled to find his way into the future, the more I recoiled from it. I began to back away from him too, and from my grown children, because loving was becoming too painful, because it made me want to grasp on to things that can't be held. My withdrawal was a form of dying, really. Willful. Private. Just a little bit every day; just enough to get the hang of it; not enough for anyone to speak up about, especially me.

As far as the rest of the world knew, I was leading an enviable and adventurous life. My bio was a good read, filled with strong words, except that for me, their energy, their sweet force, had leached out.

If I had to pick one incident to illustrate the state of my spirits, I would choose something that happened a couple of months ago during an early summer trek I was guiding in the newly opened kingdom of Mustang in Nepal—a trip I had been dreaming about doing for thirteen years.

We had climbed up the Tey Khola River bed to visit Ludi Gompa, an ancient monastery, nearly hidden in one of the many caves that pock the cliff walls of a high, uninhabited valley. It was an astonishing place, as wild and strange as any on earth.

I was feeling restless and removed as I explored the dark shrine rooms, even though I was chancing upon incredible treasures: deities draped in tiger skins, stomping on demons and copulating with their consorts; Buddhas and bodhisattvas waiting quietly in the darkness until the last sentient being passes into Nirvana. *What is the matter with me?* I wondered as I moved from room to room like a sleepwalker.

I had hoped that returning to Nepal would recharge me. But it wasn't happening, even at Ludi Gompa. At one point, I crawled up through an opening into what was left of a room with a spectacular view of the valley. A meditation room probably. Once inside, I seated myself cross-legged on the floor, just as others had been doing for thousands of years. I tried to focus my mind, but it just skipped along the surface of the moment like a flat stone on water. Down below I saw David on the steep path, his head hidden by a large black hood. He was shooting pictures of the monastery with a large-format camera. I understood then that I was going through Nepal just like that camera: recording what was there without responding to it, without feeling it.

Shame and loss scuttled through my body. In my mind I saw a line of dark-haired women winding their way down the mountain path below me. Identical forms, moving in single file: hair swinging with each step, day packs thudding softly. They pivoted slowly at each switchback, one by one, their trekking skirts flaring slightly. All those women, all those selves, leaving me. The daughter, the wanderer, the aviator. The stepmother, the divorcée, the single mother. The English teacher, the lover, the adventurer. I'd driven them all away.

I returned from that trip depleted, not sure I would ever go back to Nepal. David and I drifted erratically into the heart of the summer, lovers one day, adversaries the next. Both roles made us sad. It was David who broke through first. "I've been an Episcopal priest all my adult life," he said one day as if he had just been hit over the head with it. "When you're a priest, you can never stop being one. Not for a moment. People won't let you." And then, without another word, he made an appointment with his bishop to give him a one-year notice.

I could not believe the way this single act quickened his step. All the logs in the jam came loose at once. His cameras leapt from the upstairs closet, and swags of dripping negatives began looping back and forth in the guest bathroom, like Tibetan prayer flags. He started climbing the local ski hill every day to get in shape for a trip to the Tetons. He bought a computer, a box of pastels. His sermons became more vigorous and poetic than ever. And he became infinitely gentle and focused when he was with me, knowing that I was still jammed, knowing that I did not know what I needed to do to get going again. So it was that we fell in love again, for the hundredth time.

But it was not until the end of August, two weeks ago precisely, that my own future opened up again, abruptly, like a stuck door sprung by the heft of a body. This happened during an early morning run on a shore road in Rhode Island. I had been sensing the end of summer as I jogged along: the loaded seedpods gone to amber, the bleached grasses clicking by the roadside, the erotic stench of wild grapes. And the swallows were, as my mother used to say, "ganging up on the wires." As always, this sight stirred shapeless longings. "Every year," I said out loud. "Every year!" The sound of my voice startled me. I looked back up at the birds, squinting hard, trying to decode my feelings. What is it, this feeling I get every August when the birds are getting ready to go? What do I want . . . so much? What have I lost?

As I ran on by the saltwater marshes, by the high-stepping white egrets, more words and images began to surface: a vivid language of wind and water and slant of sun, of comings and of goings. I realized that the voice I was sensing was the same one that was stirring up the birds. But for me, it was just an echo: loud enough to disturb, yet distant enough to ignore.

I slowed down. All of me, feet, thighs, hips, respirations, the convulsing of my heart. My mind grew very still. Centered up like the needle of a compass.

What I thought was lost forever was now all around me. The spare elegance. The elemental articulation of stone and blood; the forgotten world that this language alone has the power to communicate. "*This* is the real reality," I said to myself in amazement.

Beyond the marsh and the bright sea, I saw the sky deepen, rolling out its circumference like a fresh chart. Two ropes of Canada geese swung by, their cries pealing through the morning. Why not just go? Like the birds. Try out their reality for a while. See what happens.

I felt the jump start, the purr of adrenaline. Dear God, how was I ever going to explain this one, I wondered, thinking of David, my fall schedule, all the people whose lives were interwoven with mine. Then I knew it didn't matter. Suddenly I was feeling very strong. And very much alive.

September 11, my fifty-sixth birthday. Even though I have a lot left to do before I leave tomorrow, I sit quietly at my grandmother's writing desk by the French doors of our bedroom in Canton, Connecticut. During the two weeks that have passed since that run in Rhode Island, I have been reading all I can find on migration. I am haunted by an eerie scenario reported by researcher Stephen Emlen of Cornell University. Wild birds that have been detained in cages during the migratory season will face in the direction of their would-be flights and start hopping up and down. They will continue this for days, changing their headings as they complete various legs of their ghostly routes. Scientists call this "migratory restlessness." I think about the wild bird inside of me, hopping, hopping.

On the dark surface of the pond before our house, two yellow leaves drift back and forth. My dictionary tells me that *to migrate* means "to come and go with the seasons." Perhaps it is my birthday that makes the simple definition seem so auspicious. I say the words over and over like a mantra, feeling their potency, their promise.

2

Just Going

As I soar over the Hudson River in my vintage VW bus camper, the September morning sun at my back, a gravelly mix of adrenaline and guilt creeps into my system. It feels familiar. Well, I've done this before, I admit to myself, as I snap a cassette into the VW's tape deck and turn up the rear speakers. And I have always figured out a way to justify my actions to others. "I'm looking into the adventure travel business," I'd say to my children's teachers. "I need to keep up my guiding skills," I'd say to David's parishioners. "I'm studying Buddhism," I'd tell my department head. But I knew that those were just partial truths, and the unspoken responses to them rang loud and clear. *What kind of mother . . . ? What kind of wife . . . ?* The truth is, I don't know why I have to take off the way I do. I have always done it. The trade-offs are always the same: infinite guilt in exchange for unmediated freedom, one jagged tear down the center of my being in exchange for clean cold air in my face, for fire.

But then, what can we ever do to reconcile the demands of love with the demands of the spirit? Some families, such as the one I grew up in, have more trouble with this than others. Jimmy, Nicki, Jon, and I adored our parents, but this was no simple matter. Our father was the funniest man alive and also the sloppiest drunk. He was crazy about us. He read us thrilling books like *The Three Musketeers* and *The Swiss Family Robinson*. And when he had not had too many cocktails, he told outrageous true stories at the dinner table, making us reel hysterically back and forth in our mahogany chairs until our mother would tell us to settle down or we would break the chairs.

Our mother kept her head up and her mouth shut, no matter how bad things got. Even though she was not one to pick us up and crush us to her bosom, we could tell she loved us by the things she did, like the time she actually went off to a fancy party wearing the sticky blue spangle earrings my six-year-old brother made for her. We also knew she loved our father as much as we did, which may explain why she joined him for a few awful years in his alcoholic cocoon.

Maybe it was the unruliness of love that made me take off by myself whenever I could during childhood. Who knows, maybe it is the reason I still do it. Of this I'm sure: I work hard to keep this part of me hidden because I know it scares the people who love me. It frightens me too, but in a different way. Like the way it feels to sit in the open door of an airplane, head stretched out, goggles chattering against my cheekbones, the mute earth sliding by underneath. When the pilot cuts the engine for the exit, there is abject silence, a pause so powerful, all choices are neutralized. Then you just go, that's all. Just go.

I feel "just gone" right now. Pablo Casals is playing the Bach suites, his cello modulating the flow of my blood. I trace the course of the music through my body, a squeeze at my wrists, a bounce at the nape of my neck, a cresting behind my eyes. He is playing the landscape too. Green hills heave and fold, billow up again.

Sitting high above the road in my captain's chair, armrests down, cruise control switched on, I celebrate having the bus all to myself. When David and I go on vacation in it, we painstakingly divvy up every inch of storage space. Now my laptop and bird books fill the chest reserved for his cameras; my tape recorder, cassette case, Books on Tape, and binoculars sit beside me on the passenger seat. My clothes have cavorted into all three bins under the couch/pull-out bed that runs along the driver's side.

The bus's decor is southwestern. Zigzagging soft yellows, multiple blues, and salmon pinks for the curtains, the couch, and its pillows. The backseat, covered in slate blue tweed, serves as a second couch and as a headboard at nighttime. A wooden storage chest quadruples as coffee table, footrest, and dinner table when the weather is bad. In the far back over the engine, the kitchen gear is stowed for easy access through a large hatchback door. All in all, it is a fine traveling machine for two, and for one, a Waldorf on wheels.

I've brought a map of the United States, campground guides, and the names of birding hot spots on migration flyways from one coast to the other, along with the telephone numbers of friends I may or may not call along the way. The shape I have imposed on the next five weeks has been penciled in very lightly, because what I need right now is *not* to know where I am going. That is, if I am going to learn what this trip is really about.

And this is the way I learn, by experiencing. Words, those of others as well as my own, have never been enough for me. It was hard on my parents having a child who had to jump off things, go swimming when the waves were too big, sneak out at night just to roam, test the thin ice, touch the fire, disappear for hours so that she could dream her stories without interruption and often act them out. It has been hard on my children having such a mother.

I head south through the Poconos, now on a straight course toward Hawk Mountain Sanctuary in Pennsylvania, my first stop on the eastern flyway. I'm thinking about the different ways I have managed to jump-start my life in the past. Some were theatrical, like throwing myself out of airplanes, and some more subtle, like committing myself to teach a course on something I knew nothing about.

Or popping a quarter for a phone call into the pocket of my running shorts and heading out of Canton on foot to run outbound until I dropped. One time I ran all the way through the town of West Simsbury and after that Simsbury, and then I ran up the long slope of Talcott Mountain in the steaming noonday heat. When I reached my mother's house on top of the mountain, I hooked a left, peeling off my putrid shirt as I tore down the long driveway through the woods. I toed off my Nikes as I passed through the garden, hopped out of my shorts on the wide lawn, and dove into her pool without breaking my stride. Moments later, as I lay on my back, cooling my burning scalp, my mother appeared at the side of the pool bearing a white terry cloth robe. "You may need this," she said tactfully, her kinetic blue eyes sparking with amusement as she laid the garment carefully over the arm of a metal chair.

And there were those chiseled autumn nights when I felt compelled to sleep out on the front deck of our house so I could feel the earth spinning through the universe. This one always worked, even though it horrified my kids when they were in elementary school. Anee (pronounced Ah'-nee) and Mandy lived in terror that I would oversleep and their car pool would arrive to find me lying in my sleeping bag for all the world to see, like a huge green slug. In those days it was hard enough to have a single mother, not to mention one who slept outside.

But sometimes I get so blunt nothing can sharpen me, except to go. So I construct the most plausible story I can and then disappear. Fast. Before I change my mind.

When I first told David that I wanted to take the camper and drive around the country for a few weeks to think and write about migrating birds, his handsome blue eyes grew quite merry. "Well then," he had said, without missing a beat in the conversation, "I'd better get you a new set of tires!" I think he was glad to see me brighten up after so long. And I suspect he knows me better than I think he does.

But I know that was not how he was feeling this morning when I left. Last night was very long for both of us. I could tell by the angle of his head that he too was watching the stippled moon sail through the high Palladian windows of our bedroom, but my coming departure had sealed our lips like a contract. At dawn, we made love very carefully, watching each other's faces, distilling our apprehensions down and down until they became one singular shared blind spot. Afterward, we lay side by side, looking up at the ceiling. There wasn't anything to say, really. I was already rolling west in my head, and he knew it. When we finally got out of bed, his eyes were blunt, fixed into an expression of resignation that was difficult for me to own.

"Enough of that," I say out loud, trying to shake David out of my mind. I crank the volume on the tape deck louder and louder until it fills me all the way up. *This is the way I want to feel,* I think as the strands of notes become green and deep, splashed with sunshine. Every moment a first time, a unique triangulation of time and place . . . and me. Although I have driven this road several times before, I have never been precisely here before. This landscape consists of Pablo Casals' cello and four turkey vultures riding the ribbon of warm air rising from the highway. Concrete forms for abstractions my mind can only grope at: the wings and blood, the blue and black and float and soar, the aching beauty.

3

Aloft

At least a hundred people perch on the northernmost outcrop of Hawk Mountain Sanctuary. To the birds, up there in the icy rivers of the sky, we must look like periwinkles latched to a clump of tidal rocks.

I have mixed feelings about being here. I'm not a birder, not like these folks with their scopes and high-end binoculars and sensible earth-colored clothes that minimize their presence on this famous hawk flyway. My screaming-blue mountaineering parka makes me feel like some kind of toxin. I knew this was one of the key migration hot spots in the country—in fact, Hawk Mountain Sanctuary was one of the first to protect migrating birds—but at the moment I am longing for something a bit more solitary.

Besides, I woke up tired this morning after a fitful first night in the bus. Without realizing it, I had parked so that my head was pointing slightly downhill, and I spent most of the night trying to decide whether it bothered me enough to get out of my warm sleeping bag and do something about it. I won't do that again.

*   *   *

"Bald eagle over point five," the Hawk Mountain Sanctuary naturalist calls out, just as I am getting settled on my boulder. I rummage frantically through my pack for my binoculars. The eagle works his way toward us, riding the north-south-ridge lift of the Kittatinny Mountains. Once everybody gets fastened on to him, all motion ceases on the outcropping except for the barely perceptible sweep of one hundred binoculars. He passes close, maybe fifty feet above us and a little to the left, his patrician head turned toward us, black eyes canny, yellow beak open, as if he were about to pontificate, or perhaps to scream. A slow groan of pleasure passes from person to person, the volume building as we rotate with him. "Ohhhhhhhhhh," we say. When we finally lower our glasses, we sit looking around at one another, dumbfounded. Someone begins to clap. A leather and wool glove-cupping sound spreads over the rocky knoll. What else can you do?

The broad-wing hawks come in next, spiraling toward the cloud bases in towering kettles so they can take advantage of the winds aloft. One stops his flight right above the edge of the cliff. Just stops. Then he presses his hefty wings flat against his body and stoops, dropping by us like a shot-put into the valley below. Our binoculars plummet with him. "Wowwwwwwwww," we moan together.

The birds come and come and come, specks surfacing above the horizon like fireflies out of a summer twilight. Ospreys and kestrels, Cooper's hawks and sharp-shins. We count them all, each one igniting a fresh hunger. We count the monarch butterflies too. And the warblers. At one point, during a lull, a young boy notes a strange beetle sitting on a bush and calls out, "Dad, look at that bug!" One hundred binoculars fall ecstatically upon the poor creature, who was just trying to eat his lunch in peace.

During the noon lull, I lie back against my pack, close my eyes, and try to place this day in a context of natural time. The birds I have been observing all morning are tuned in to an infinitely complicated set of forces: the failing light, the sudden and substantial weight they have just gained, the recent low-pressure system that was followed by a swift cold front, the ridge patterns below them, the life cycles of their prey, the angle of the sun in relation to the zenith, the magnetic poles of the earth, and the urgent voices of their ancestors, who, like trees falling in the forest without witness, flew these routes in a seamless time before the mind of man.

This is my story too, I think as I shield my eyes and scan the horizon to the north. I just don't understand why my mind keeps fighting it. Keeps choosing to operate in a constricted moment, a blanket over its head, when it could just as easily opt for the exhilarating sweep of natural time.

The sun is moving off the rocks, and people have begun to leave. I relocate on a large flat rock to take advantage of the last warm rays. Even though the birds have slowed down, I am reluctant to leave any of the afternoon unmined. I lie flat on my back, looking up at the high cirrus clouds overhead. Suddenly, a large red-tailed hawk inserts himself in the foreground of my circle of vision. I hold still and so does he, filling up my glasses. "A local," the naturalist reports. I have never seen wind finger the belly down of a hawk before, never seen a sunset through russet tail feathers, never seen the gleaming white aura of a warm body suspended in the sky, wings absolutely motionless, balancing rather than flying. Someone makes a joke: "That's Abigail" is what he says. A breathy chuckle erupts from the crowd; we all have been holding our breath. The hawk does not twitch, and we stay glued to it while another minute passes. Then the naturalist calls out to us, "Better take a good last look, I'm going to cut the string." We laugh again. Breathe again. No one can believe this.

When at last the hawk sails on down the ridge, I turn to a man sitting near me. "How long do you think it was there?" I ask. He grins and shakes his head. "I don't know. At least three or four minutes. A lifetime."

The campground near the sanctuary has just a few sites, all filled with birders. I back the bus into my space this time, so my head will be higher than my feet.

The green-and-white-checked tablecloth I spread over the picnic table quickly transforms the rather featureless pull-out into a pleasant green bower. On it, I place a jar full of pink cosmos and blue salvia from my garden at home. I set up my kitchen at one end of the table, the Coleman stove, a five-gallon water jug, a crate of pots and pans and utensils. A cutting board. A tray of spices. Two candle lanterns.

Then I locate a black Magic Marker and my map of the United States. I'm ready to make some decisions. I circle Chincoteague National Wildlife Refuge off the coast of eastern Virginia, a key staging area for birds heading down the eastern flyway. I put a question mark over Virginia because I have not decided whether I have the energy or the courage to call Ben. I make a big bold circle over central Kansas, where lies a very big marsh called Cheyenne Bottoms, which, according to my books, should be crammed with migrating birds about now. Then I underline the Colorado Springs airport. I have already bought a plane ticket to fly round-trip from there to California to visit my friend Rachel and check out the West Coast flyway. Finally I make three circles that are pretty close together: Taos, New Mexico, where my twenty-nine-year-old daughter, Anee, lives, and two birding hot spots in southern Colorado, where, if everything goes perfectly, I will see the fabled sandhill cranes, migrating down the Rocky Mountain flyway. This is enough, I say to myself, looking at my unconnected dots. Bare bones, anyway. *Of what?* I wonder. *My next life?*

After pouring a glass of white wine and adding to it the few cubes left in my ice chest, I begin sautéing crimini mushrooms, red peppers, and onions. When they soften a bit, I add arborio rice, some chicken broth, some of the wine, and finally some sugar snap peas from the fall crop in my garden. Because the sky is empty of clouds, the sun departs without giving notice, yellow orange green gone. Then radiant pink, deep lavender. When I light the candle lanterns, the great purple globe around my table goes blue-black. Like the ink. Only the bellying treetops surrounding the campground are darker than the sky. I let the light go without protest; I am so filled with it right now. It makes me feel transparent, like bright glass, like a window open wide.

I crawl into my sleeping bag early, eager to let the images of the day go free in my mind. Touching the face of the wind, dark wings flex and ease. They read the wisps of clouds forming above them, the dark heaves of the mountains below. Now the sudden bounce of a thermal, now the yank of a downdraft. The birds of my mind tilt and swing as I lie in the blue bus, until finally, their taut wings bank up against the wind and they streak out of my head, peeling off one by one, like canoes that have been pointing upstream, arcing back into the roll of the river.

I think about the caves high up in the white cliff faces of Nepal, the ones used for air burial. With binoculars you can see the stone platforms where Tibetan Buddhists spread out the chopped-up remains of their loved ones for the birds to pick clean. You do not need binoculars to see the huge elegant birds, wheeling in dark coils over the burial caves, over the snowcapped peaks, all the way up to 20,000 feet.

"Instant reincarnation," I say to myself as I drift toward sleep. "One could do worse."

4

Solo

Heading south toward Maryland after a nine-hour "power sleep," as my kids call it. When I crawled out of the bus this morning at first light, the sharp cold air surprised me. I pumped up the stove as fast as I could, put on the coffeepot, and stomped around impatiently as it came to a boil. Then I hopped back into my still warm sleeping bag. Bliss is the only word for it: a toasty goosedown bag, a steaming mug of Sumatra coffee, the ruddy sun prowling through the trees, dark birds flitting, leaf sounds, grass smells.

Time alone, I thought as I slowly sipped my coffee, *has a different texture, a greater density*.

This was the topic of several conversations I had had with David before I left. One took place on a rainy Sunday afternoon on my mother's old camelback couch in our family lair. Feet up on the table, half-buried by an eruption of newspapers, I was eagerly devouring *The Random House Atlas of Bird Migration*, yet another present from David.

"You must love me!" I had announced suddenly. "Why else

would you put up with someone who's chomping at the bit to get away from you?"

"Thanks a lot," he had answered, scruffing up my hair. "That really helps." Then he added in a more serious tone, "I just know that there are times when you need to get off by yourself."

"You say that so matter-of-factly. I've always felt guilty about it. Like it was something I had to hide."

Then he asked a question that took me by surprise. "Why do you need so much time alone? Do you know?"

"I've never thought about it . . ." I answered haltingly. "Only about how to get away with it. And I've been trying to do that all my life. It wasn't easy with three other hawk-eyed kids in the family. But I had my methods."

I went on to tell him how, as a child, I would get up very early in the morning, before anyone else was awake. How I would dress in my closet, negotiate the creaks of the stairs as if they were land mines, and then, handle held all the way over to the right, ever so carefully shut the screen door.

Once free of the house, I would take off in the blue half-light like a little sparrow, flitting from yard to yard to yard. In the privacy of the dawn hour, the world of our West Hartford neighborhood and Elizabeth Park beyond was hushed and sacred, filled with wonders that were mine alone. I remembered a wheelbarrow heaped with new snow that cupped my six-year-old body like a hand. I lay in it for a long time, waiting for the light, watching quarter-sized snowflakes weave a thick blanket over me, thinking happily that this must be how dead people feel, cozy there in the snow and the dark.

I went on to tell him about another time, also before sunup, when I found a rope swing in the backyard of a neighbor we did not know. It was too high for me to reach, so I climbed up the tree and jumped for it. The rope was covered with ice. My collarbone snapped like a dead twig when I hit the frozen ground.

"It's funny, I've been so busy trying to conceal my behavior, I've never thought about why I am the way I am. Both of my parents were only children. Maybe that has something to do with it . . . because it looks like they produced *four* only children."

"I'm not sure I know what that means," David responded.

I wasn't exactly sure myself; I had never thought of myself as an only child before. Then I recalled what a friend of mine, who really was an only child, had told me years ago. At that time I had been worrying about the fact that my mother was spending so much time by herself up there on her hilltop. My father had been dead for more than fifteen years. My friend told me that being alone was my mother's natural state, the time when she felt most at ease, at home.

After telling David this, I added, "Think about us. We are all just like her, really."

"Yeah, it's true," he confirmed, shaking his head in wonder. "Which is strange because you all seem so different, at least on the surface."

It was true. Jimmy, the oldest, who was divorced years ago, seems to have adapted well to living alone. And when my younger sister, Nicki, met Sam, a solitary man much like her, she moved with him to a remote area of Connecticut where they now thrive on isolation, birds and bears and bobcats, their orchards and their gardens. The youngest one, Jon, who is an engineer turned carpenter, is just like the rest of us: a bit shy outside the family circle, happy to spend large chunks of the day alone working without interruptions, independent to the point of being quirky.

David chuckled. "It really is amazing that you all get

along so well, given the fact that the four of you are so fiercely independent."

"That one goes back a long way in the Batterson family. It's not our fault—really," I said sheepishly.

"It's a wonder you all found enough elbow room to grow up . . . without maiming each other."

"I don't know about the others," I replied, "but what I do know is that it was during my dawn roamings that I felt the most whole. Like I was a part of an intentional, orderly universe." I paused to absorb what I had just said. David was nodding his head almost imperceptibly; I could tell he was right with me. And then it came to me. Solitude, for me, was an elemental need, like water or love. I was my parents' child. That's all. There was nothing to feel guilty about. Was there?

I turned to David. "I used to think that if I was ever lucky enough to have a really healthy relationship, I wouldn't need so much time to myself. And that has turned out to be true . . . up to a point. Our relationship depends on the fact that we both can feel alone when we are together. Do you agree?"

He nodded. "That's very important to me too. But you said 'up to a point.' What point?"

"I believe that there is a place in all of us that is ours alone, that we never share, ever. Not with each other, not with our kids, not with our closest friends. I'm talking about the quick: the part of me that fell in love with you, the part that splits open like a milkweed pod when I listen to *Madame Butterfly*."

I take a breath and home in closer. "I'm talking about the part that wakes up terrified in the middle of the night. That believes or doesn't believe in God. And, in the end, it's the part of us that must confront and *live out* our most singular of deaths. It's like a deep spring, hidden, vital. And when it runs low, as mine does sometimes, no one can replenish it but me."

We sat in silence for a while. Then David responded, "Well,

I'm not so sure about the last thing you said . . . For me, that's what a spiritual life is all about—replenishing. Trusting that there is more to all of this than just me."

"My problem is that when I get really low, I don't have a spiritual life."

"That's not how it's supposed to work," he answered gently. "We all need some buffer between ourselves and the void. You can't just stand there gaping at it."

"Well, I certainly have been giving it my full attention," I said. As I reached out to touch his face, I added, "Surely I must have something better to do."

I have returned to this conversation several times in the past week. Each time I experience a new spaciousness, a widening in my chest. I think about my mother, how the silence of her house and the land she lived on must have felt like a comfortable old robe to her. I shudder to think what she went through every time I showed up at the family cottage in Rhode Island with five kids, an au pair, a Great Dane, a garbage-eating boxer named Gino who wasn't even ours, and two or three hysterical cats.

All of a sudden, I am back in our old red station wagon driving into Hartford. Anee and Mandy, age seven and four, are strapped into the backseat. Just as we approach The Orphanage—always a high point of this trip—I hear Anee whisper to herself, "Grandma was a lonely child."

I don't correct her pronunciation because I'm curious to hear what will come next. She remains silent until we are just abreast of The Orphanage. Then I hear a deep sigh, and a tiny voice saying, "Look, Mandy, that's where all the lonely children live."

5

Dead Reckoning

The bridge over Chesapeake Bay thrusts me high into the blue vault of the afternoon. Now eyeball to eyeball with dense white gulls, I turn up the volume of the tape deck as high as it will go. Pavarotti belts out, *"Nessun dorma! Nessun dorma!"* I sing along at the top of my lungs. The world is awake. Nobody sleeps!

When the car phone rings, I nearly jump out the window.

"Hi," says David, sounding equally startled. "I just thought I'd try the new phone. Where are you, the Met?"

"Hold on. Let me turn it off." I reach over and eject Luciano. "Somewhere east of the Chesapeake. Where are you?"

"Home. Just got back from church. I had a bunch of meetings after the service."

"Oh yeah. Sunday. What did you preach on—what to do when your wife runs away with a bird?"

He laughs. "I might as well have. Nobody listens to sermons anyway."

"Yes they do, David," I chide as always. "They listen to yours. They really do."

"Oh well," he sighs, and then changing the subject, "What's it like there?"

"It's gorgeous. A perfect afternoon to drive to the coast. What are you going to do with the rest of your day?"

"I'm not sure. I picked up the *New York Times*."

I can see him standing in the kitchen. His tall, trim form bending over the kitchen table, pulling out the Sunday magazine, the book review, and the travel section from the smooth fresh mound, pushing back his forelock of straight blond hair, the one that slips down onto his brow when he bows his head to kiss me, or to bless the communion wine. I see his hands, small and nimble like a surgeon's, his fingers beautifully milled. David's hands, deftly chopping parsley, modulating the eye of his camera, contouring my waist, hip, and thigh, the lightest touch, cool, dry, full.

"I'm starting to miss you," I say abruptly, trying to cut off the sensation of his hands, and too, the vision of the endless Sunday afternoon unfurling before him. These images, I bulldoze quickly.

"I miss you very much," he replies simply, without accusation. "Call me when you get settled tonight."

After we say good-bye the bus feels empty, like a sail suddenly let go. It was wonderful to have him here in this space with me, zooming along in the sunshine. I love being around David. Even though we have been married for nine years, it seems like months. We are still a bit in awe of each other. Afraid of screwing up. This is no small matter. My first marriage was so cataclysmic, I shut down my heart for fourteen years. Except for the part where my children grew and thrived.

My emotions begin to snarl. There is nothing I can do to spare David from the next few weeks. "Some minister's wife," I mutter out loud, feeling horribly self-serving.

That's the price tag, I remind myself.

Last Sunday, I panicked on my way to coffee hour after the service. What was I going to say to everyone? But then what can I ever say?

I'm sorry I am late for church every single Sunday, no matter how hard I try. And I do try. You should see me putting on lipstick in the rearview mirror, writing my pledge check on the rotating air bag unit at the center of the steering wheel, patting my black wool coat all over with a wad of Scotch tape to get the dog hairs off. I've often wondered how I looked from the back. Like a yeti probably.

And I'm even sorrier about the bishop's last visit to our parish. I didn't realize anything was amiss until coffee hour after the service. I was introducing the bishop's wife to an elderly parishioner when I first noticed I was listing to port. When I finally had a chance to look down, I saw one black shoe; the other one was very blue, and they weren't even the same height. To make matters much worse, an absurd giddiness took possession of my senses. I was a shambles. The only thing I could think to do was to point to my feet. "Heh, heh, heh" is what I muttered helplessly.

But what can you expect from someone who was Episcopalian at birth, an agnostic in high school, an existentialist in college, a druid in midlife, and a Buddhist for the long haul. No one was more surprised than I was to learn that I had fallen wildly in love with a priest. He showed up for our first date wearing Levi's, a gray herringbone tweed jacket, cruddy cowboy boots, and a clerical collar—apologizing that he had not had time to change out of his work clothes. The combination was irresistible. Kissing a man in a clerical collar was a singular kind of experience for me. Still is.

What bothers me now, however, is the fact that, for some time, I have felt restless and trapped during services. That I don't know what I believe anymore. Or don't believe.

David knows all of this. And if it bothers him, he doesn't say. He listens to me as a friend would, not a priest. From the time we fell in love, he has insisted that we separate our life together from his job. Although it isn't always easy for me to do that—especially when I get focused on other people's expectations—I have come to understand that he needs a lover and a companion much more than he needs a minister's wife. The key to this is parity. I support what he does with his life. He supports what I do with mine.

I must confess a part of me still refuses to believe that he is real. Yet every time I probe him, as I am doing right now, I find out how much I underestimate him.

Early evening. I still have an hour or two before I reach the coast. While the Chincoteague National Wildlife Refuge is actually on the island of Assateague, I will have to camp on Chincoteague Island where there are services for human visitors.

The fields around me, now cleared of crops, present a rolling sea of stubble, seeds, and grasses. Starlings crest and curl in waves. Stately three-story houses appear and disappear like great slow ships. As the light fails, the scene grows still, becomes permanent, except for the rise and fall of the birds.

The towns are narrow; only a few houses line up beside the main road. Street signs say things like Toadvine, Nutterhill, Sapperhollow, another language here.

When I stopped for gas a few minutes ago, I was surprised to find out that my presence qualified as news. A sidelong glance. Eye contact between two men leaning against a counter. A backward roll of the head. Just enough to transform the euphoric me of bright afternoon into a lone woman driving a VW bus at nightfall in someone else's town.

I stop at a grocery store, pick up a small roasted chicken, some tarnished lettuce, and a tomato. A minor errand, but it steadies me.

Seven-thirty P.M. A viscous density without stars or moon. Nothing was open in the last two towns. People were locked up in their houses, curtains pulled against the darkness, against the idea of strangers roaming through their towns. The only sign of life was the pale blue light of television sets pooling in parlor windows. Nothing more.

I can tell I am nearing the coast because the night air feels gummy and smells like the sea. Another ghostly village has just slipped away. No lights anywhere. Rows of houses, standing like tombstones, along the main road, shoulder to shoulder, expressionless. Where is everybody? My headlights barely dent the huge night before me. Out here a person could drive right off the edge of the continent, arc into the night sea, and disappear like a pebble. My body tenses, releases, tenses again.

This is the outward-bound edginess of pilots who fly in remote and featureless spaces, I remind myself, taking in a deep slug of clammy air. I used to feel it every time I flew single-engine-over-water charters to the "outer islands" in the Bahamas. Because there were no landmarks after the island of Freeport, and no navigational aids at my destination to home in on, I had to navigate by dead reckoning, a method based on time and speed and heading rather than fixed reference points. This is a breath-stopping way to navigate; without landmarks, you never really know where you are until you get there. *Sounds like the story of my life*, I mutter to myself as I strain into the darkness before me, looking for the lights of Chincoteague Island.

*   *   *

This so-called campground has given muscle to all sorts of apprehensions. Although it's filled with pull-trailers and large RVs, there is absolutely no one here. The only light shines over the office door where a note Scotch-taped to the glass demands PAY IN THE MORNING. The other campgrounds I checked out were either closed or deserted like this one. Evidently people from the cities leave their recreational vehicles here for weekend use during the fall. "Midweek and out of season," I mutter to myself. "That's me."

Afraid that my interior lights might attract unwanted attention, I back the blue bus between two large vehicles near the back of the campground.

Dinner is not the word for it. Too out of sorts to unload the cooking gear, I sever a slab of breast meat from the chicken and roll it up in a piece of pita bread. "This isn't what I had in mind," I say to the night. I'm glad no one can see me right now, the great adventurer, cowering in an RV park, wishing she were home in her bed.

My sandwich is too dry to swallow. Mayonnaise is what I need. I wrap it up in a paper napkin and stuff it in a trash bag. I feel stupid. Solitude and loneliness are two sides of the same event, separated by a heartbeat only. Solitude is what I was talking about with David before I left; loneliness is what looms at me right now. And it is not a pretty sight. There have been times in my adult life when it has stung me into a stupor, when it has encased me in its cement and dropped me in the drink.

Loneliness is not something to play around with, I say to myself as I grab the corner of a curtain and yank it over the gaping black hole beside me. This helps. I switch on my new battery-powered overhead lamp. Then I quickly seal up the rest of the windows, lay out my sleeping bag on the couch, fluff up two down pillows, and place the car phone, my alarm clock, and a glass of cranberry iced tea on the chest where I can easily reach them.

Now, nesting in eiderdown, my laptop on my knees, I feel a little better. The lamp drops a warm pool of light over me, making my little room quite cozy. I learned recently that night migrators, the small birds who use the cover of darkness for protection against predators, emit a continuous stream of peeps and pipes to keep in touch with one another. I feel like one of those tiny birds now, piping away in the darkness. I am very tired, but I don't want to stop writing. It keeps me fastened to the world, and it keeps the lonely ghosts outside the bus. I had forgotten about them, about the fact that there was a time, between the ages of twenty and twenty-six, that they were my most frequent traveling companions.

6

The Journey Within
the Journey

It is not surprising that the memory of my first solo journey across the country would surface here in this deserted campground in Virginia. The old ghosts are always out there circling, just beyond the edge of whatever order we have managed to create in our lives. The purpose of that trip had been to leave home, but I didn't have any place to go, really.

At twenty-two just going meant momentum only. That is, until I got to Las Vegas. I had stopped there because it was in my path, or more important, because my sole contact in Los Angeles, which was as far from home as I could get, was "out of town for a week," as her roommate told me when I tried to reach her by phone.

Upon arrival, I drove out to "The Strip" to see the famous casinos. That took ten minutes. My heart dropped into my sneakers when I realized there wasn't anything else to see. After a desultory trip to the other end of town, I checked into a nondescript one-story motel, paid for four days, and fell asleep without waking for dinner.

At 6:15 A.M., I woke up very hungry. Showering quickly, I

braided my hair wet, pulled on jeans and a sweatshirt, and went out to find an all-night diner I had spotted the day before. As I worked my way through a stack of pancakes, I read the local paper from front to back, ads and all. Then I did the crossword puzzle. Then I returned to the motel. My wind-up Big Ben said 7:30 A.M.

I remember clearly the six-inch strip of light angling into the room through a slot between the rust-stained curtains. In it, motes of dust tumbled and drifted like atoms. I remember, too, feeling perplexed by the fact that the light did not spread out into the gloom, that it stayed obediently within the borders of its shaft, as if it had been colored in with a gold crayon.

I sat down on the bed. The ticking of Big Ben grew louder and louder, filling up the remaining space around the spike of light. The small pile of books I had placed on the bedside table was there for the sole purpose of making the room seem inhabited. I had read them all, except for my grandmother's hardbound edition of *War and Peace*, which I didn't have the heart for just then. Through the open window, I could hear the rhythmic dopplering of passing cars, hissing softly like waves seething on a beach.

The panic arrived in waves too, mounting steadily as I confronted the empty hours stacking up before me.

I began grilling myself. How is it possible to have absolutely nothing to do? No place to go? No one to talk to? What happened to my life?

Two years before to the day, I had been in Italy, emoting over Masaccio's frescoes and making large, disorderly paintings. After that, an unraveling: a boring clerical job in New York City. Ski-bumming jobs in Vermont and Colorado. An impulsive dash to Acapulco. Then, during a fateful pause, I had landed at home in Connecticut to find that the world I had left behind when I went away to college, the world that had provided both my security and the basis of my freedom, was disintegrating. My father's drinking had escalated alarmingly in the brief years that I'd been away. And his early retirement from the corporate world had been a mistake. Instead of buying the old boatyard he had always talked about, or starting a company that made model sailboats that would *really* sail (another much-discussed venture), he ended up sitting on the couch most of the time, slowly sipping bourbon, smoking one cigarette after another and sometimes two at a time, and disappearing a little bit every day, along with his dreams. To make matters worse, my mother was disappearing with him. I hung around, thinking my presence might help somehow. I listened to the house, marked the bottles, even posted myself beside the liquor cabinet with a book. Finally I went to our family doctor for help. He said he could do nothing unless my parents asked for it themselves. I tried to talk with my father. I'd say, "You're still young. Don't do this to yourself, to Mother, to us." I'd say, "What about the boatyard?" He would listen to me carefully, tear up a bit, and take a sip. Then, his eyes growing distant, he would say in a soft, sad voice that I was too young to understand, that I needed to concentrate on my own life.

I started to blame myself. Maybe I had stayed away too long. Maybe I had been too wild, too selfish. After several months, I left for "the West" because I could not help them, and they could not help me.

Sitting there on the edge of my bed in that crummy motel in Las Vegas, I realized that I had passed a point of no return, that I had let go of all my reasons to turn around: friendships, passions, purposes. I began to fixate on the memory of an old man who lived in a house where I had rented a room one summer. On my return from breakfast every morning, I would see him through his partially open door, sitting on the edge of his bed, eyes straight ahead, feet on the floor. I could tell by the slump of his shoulders and the slack of his arms that he would remain exactly there until it was time for lunch. This knowledge had terrified me every time I passed his door. I used to lie awake at night agonizing about him, despising myself for my inability to acknowledge him with so much as a smile or a wave.

There in the stillness of my twenty-second year, I felt the resolute sag of my own shoulders. I looked down at my veiny hands, dangling loose between my knees just like the old man's. That was the moment that time fell flat on its face. Right before my eyes. It was a stunning moment, one I have never gotten over. It fills me with terror even now. Especially now.

I have no memory of the rest of that day in the motel. That was probably the day I met the gypsy woman in the Laundro-mat, who ended up following me for days, frightening me so much that I left town in the middle of the night. I never knew whether she was after my body or my car or my friendship, but I doubt it was the latter. She was, I think, something inevitable. Given the fact that I was in Las Vegas. Given the void in my life.

But a void like that doesn't just curl up and die when you leave a place. It hops right in the car with you. So I'd found out a little later that same night, when I lost a headlight as I was weaving through the mountains heading for the Califor-nia border. It was very dark and I couldn't see the curves until I was upon them. When a car passed me, I realized that its headlights solved my problem, so I stepped on the gas to keep up with it. After about an hour of this, I began to feel sleepy, so I dropped back and turned into an all-night truck stop.

While I was sitting on a stool at the counter drinking

coffee, a hand appeared on my shoulder. "Lost your left head-light, huh?"

"How'd you know?" I asked, spinning my stool around to find a large pock-faced man, probably in his late thirties, standing behind me. Wearing a spattered blue T-shirt, painter pants, and work boots, he looked as if he had just come off a job.

"You've been following me for an hour," he replied, sliding onto the stool next to mine. "Where you going?"

"California," I muttered politely, picking up my bill and putting my purse over my shoulder. I was beginning to feel uneasy. He had been ahead of me when I turned off the road. He must have turned around and come back to find me. He reached out and snatched the bill out of my hand.

"Oh, you don't have to do that, I've got it," I sputtered.

"No problem," he responded, shaking his head, his lips parting in a loose, wet smile. He was missing one of his front teeth.

"Well, I gotta go. Thanks." I started for the door.

"Wait up," he said, leaving some money on the counter. "I'll lead you until it's light."

"You don't have to do that," I said lamely.

"I know that," he responded, holding the door for me, his face uncomfortably close.

But the night wore on without incident. We were out on the open desert when it grew light. All of a sudden, he pulled over, signaling dramatically for me to stop. I thought some-thing was wrong with my car; maybe the other headlight had gone out. I walked up to where he was parked and said, "What's wrong?"

He sat in the driver's seat, looking up at me, an obscure mirth jiggering his features. Then he clamped his left hand around my wrist.

"I just thought we might, you know." He swung his head toward the backseat of his car. "Get in."

"Oh, no. This is a mistake. You misunderstood me," I stammered. "You were really nice to help me out, but—" His hand tightened on my wrist, and I saw something that looked like anger jerking around in his eyes.

"Jesus God! Let me go. Please!" I pleaded.

He was clearly struggling with himself; his lips, still parted, had ceased to smile. He ran his eyes up and down my body, ending at my neck each time. Frantic, I looked around. The desert swept out to the horizons like the sea. Empty. "For God's sake. Please!"

He let go abruptly, flinging my arm back at me like something dead. Without looking at me again, he started up his car and peeled off fast, spraying sand and gravel all over my legs. For several seconds I just stood there, adrenaline crawling all over my skin like ants. I felt dirty, stupid. Then I ran like hell for the safety of my car.

I have not thought about that journey for many years. The way my life collapsed without warning. The vacancy that took its place was like a black hole, attracting everything within reach . . . without discrimination. Unfortunately, the gypsy and the drifter were just preludes to the gray-haired, silver-tongued spin-meister who was to orchestrate chaos in my life for much of the next decade.

When I finally turn off the VW's overhead lamp and nestle down into my bag, I feel oddly exorcised. The present is bonded to the past by such an elusive chemistry, like a print to its negative, like the glass of a mirror to its black backing. But there is a critical difference between that trip and the one I am on now: the starting point. David. Anee. Mandy. My larger family and friends.

My travel clock tells me it is 3:15 A.M. at the RV corral on Chincoteague Island. I push the curtain aside to check the stars. A large Winnebago rears up, obscuring most of the sky. This night will be over in three hours, I tell myself. Three hours will be a snap.

7

The Great Blue Heron

Morning. A soft dawning over the Atlantic Ocean. As I drive out to the refuge, the sun steps nimbly out of the sea. Ankle deep in a shallow channel to my left, four great white egrets are frozen in midstride. On my right, a huge flock of Canada geese sways on the incoming tide, heads still tucked in tight.

Bonaparte's gulls have appropriated the sprawling parking lots beside the great barrier beach. They pay me scant attention as I bang around, pulling out the Coleman stove, the coffeepot, the bag of Sumatra coffee that I bought near Washington. Attracted by the scent of percolating coffee, a ranger fleshes out before me.

"I had a stove like that once," he says wistfully, "and I had a VW bus too." He notices the wild turkey feather hanging by its leather thong from the rearview mirror. "A beauty. New England," he concludes. Refusing coffee with another sigh, he goes off to collect the garbage bags from the containers on the periphery of the parking lot. I take my cup of coffee up onto the dunes. Last night's dark visitors have receded with the light. Here on the primordial beach, drinking strong coffee, feeling the sun creep into my pile jacket, here I am central, opaque, in place.

Back at the bus I begin what will become a morning ritual: the bird books go into the bottom of the knapsack, then the thermos of coffee, next the peanut butter and blackberry jam sandwich made with nine-grain bread. On top, my tape recorder wrapped in an extra sweater. I attach a Crazy Creek chair to an outside loop with a climbing carabiner.

The refuge is huge, but I know it is best to pick one spot and stay there for a while. I choose a large saltwater pond just inland of the barrier beach, which is alive with migrating mallards, blue wing teals, piping swarms of shorebirds, and one large white goose. I settle into my chair, an ingenious contraption, no more than two insulated cushions with two adjustable straps, but it allows me to sit on the ground comfortably for hours. Just as I begin pouring my second cup of coffee, an enormous great blue heron drops silently out of the sky, landing in a small waterway twenty feet away. My heart stops, then begins throbbing in my neck.

The stately bird addresses me with a knowing look as she has so many times before. Then she begins to hunt, lifting and placing her legs so slowly that she does not distort her perfect image in the water.

"Slow down," she says to me as always. "Slow down."

"Okay. Okay," I murmur obediently, shaking my shoulders and exhaling forcefully. I feel chastised. I know my attention is all over the place, that I do need to settle down.

The great blue began to speak to me four years ago, shortly after my mother died. We were driving into the cemetery in formal procession. Black limousines, fresh white snow. I saw the heron first. It was standing on the ice at the mouth of a small pond, watching us pass. "What is it doing here," I asked myself, "in December?" Then something joyful moved inside of me, and I turned to my sister, Nicki. She was already smiling at me, her navy blue eyes fully charged. "It's her," she whispered softly. The news spread among the grandchildren in the other cars in a similar manner, so my sister-in-law Charlie told me later, eyes connecting, nods, smiles of acknowledgment.

My mother died during the first snowstorm of the year, lying on the camelback couch before the fire in her library. I believe she had suited up for the event: a bright pink turtleneck with "Jackson Hole" embroidered on the collar—a gift from a grandchild—her favorite gray-and-cream Icelandic sweater, and the wool kilt that went so well with it. I had spent the long winter afternoon correcting papers nearby while she snoozed on and off, chatted about Christmas presents, the coming storm, the winter light.

At one point, she asked me to change the dressing on her neck. The hospice nurse who usually did this had just called to say she had been held up. I unpacked the contents of the blue plastic basin carefully, laid them out on what looked like a disposable baby diaper: the four-by-fours of gauze, the sterile saline, the antiseptic wipes, the Q-Tips, the surgical tape. Even though I had been trained as an emergency medical technician, the prospect of touching my dying mother made me ice up with terror. Pulling on the latex gloves, I concentrated on my breathing. "Rising. Falling," I chanted inside. "Rising. Falling."

Finally I took hold of one corner of the stained bandage and eased it back very very slowly . . . until it began to cling wickedly to her neck. Grimacing hard, I lowered my arms and let out the breath I had been storing. I daubed the exposed flesh and the dark crease in the bandage gently with sterile pads drenched in saline. Pulled again.

"It's okay to go faster," she said in a light voice. "Marion just whips it off all at once."

I let out my breath again. Dropped my shoulders. "I'll try, Mom. I don't want to hurt you."

"You're doing fine, dear. I'm not as fragile as you think."

When I got one side completely free, I folded back the bandage. A musky fragrance seeped into the room. Blood? I wondered. The inside of my mother? Then I snapped the gauze away from her neck.

"You can put that in the plastic bag over there," she said, gesturing behind her with her hand. She tilted her face away from me so I could better see her assassin.

The tumor had broken out of her body about ten days ago. A deadly hollyhock, blooming below her ear.

Reverently, I began to clean the outermost petal with an antiseptic pad. Then I opened up the packet of sterile Q-Tips and spread them out before me. I entered the creases. Cradling her head with my left hand, I felt a flutter of joy as she slowly released its weight to me. I was mesmerized by the way my palm cupped her skull so easily, the way her fine hair fell loose between my fingers. She was so light. Like a bird or a balsa wood kite frame. I took my time. Twisting the cotton tips to fine points like paintbrushes, I probed deeper and deeper, exploring the fluting ridges, the deep whorls. I was rapt with the intimacy of this act. I wanted it to go on forever. She had never let me in before.

When I finished, I lay down beside her on the couch, something I had not done since I was a child. I rubbed her bony shoulder blades gently with my palms. We didn't talk anymore.

Minutes after I left that night, she died easily in Nicki's arms, assuring her that she was not afraid. When my brothers and I arrived back at the house a few minutes later, we arranged ourselves around her on her bed, creating a nest, and then we talked to her, telling jokes and stories, all the while stroking her face and hands as her spirit moved slowly away from us. After the others left the room, I recited the letter I had recently written to her, but did not give to her when she was alive, knowing how uncomfortable it would have made her feel.

> Dear Mom,
> Thank you for books.
> Thank you for music.
> Thank you for daffodils.
> Thank you for teaching me how to sit still.
> Like a hawk.

Four children and seven grandchildren carried the casket up the snowy hill to the family burial place. David led the way, his black-and-white robes billowing, his step strong and sure. The casket felt buoyant. We were exuberant, having been granted the privilege of caring for her during her illness, of holding her as she slipped away, of carrying her these last few steps of her journey and laying her in the ground. And we had seen the great blue heron.

The one before me now rotates her head slowly, holding me stock-still with her bright orange eye. Then she lifts, silhouettes for one breathless moment, and vanishes. In his book *The Dictionary of Symbols and Imagery*, Ad de Vries links the blue heron with regeneration. This does not surprise me. But there is another reference that does: "Germanic Friggia's crown had heron feathers in it to symbolize she knew all that happened on earth but kept silent about it; in icons, often with a stone in its mouth."

The noon sun slants at a disturbing angle, making the pond feel dreamlike, out of kilter. I have moved out onto a shoal to get closer to the swarms of migrating plovers, ruddy turn-stones, and sanderlings. The Audubon Society's *Master Guide to Birding* contains small blue maps that tell me these tiny, exquisitely crafted shorebirds breed in wild Arctic places, so remote and strange and lonely that it is nearly impossible to comprehend the immense design of their minute lives.

My mind floats into the map, tugged by a pale northern seascape. For a moment I sense the icy mists rising from newly thawed estuaries, the slap and suck of wave on rock, the yelp-ing of the sea lions. For a moment, a part of me remembers the cold and the wet. Perhaps we once knew these places, before we came out of the sea. How could we forget such things?

Most of the birds bobbing and skittering before me on the wet sand will fly all the way to Central and South America, crossing long, empty stretches of open water. Some, like the elegant little Arctic tern, will log up the twenty-five thousand miles in one migratory cycle as they loop from pole to pole and back again. Some are so perfectly created they don't even need to land during their migrations. Swifts, for example, leav-ing Europe in the fall, can remain on the wing, feeding on insects and floating and dreaming in the rivers of the sky, until they return to their nesting grounds nine months later, never landing. This thought makes my hair pull at my scalp. To live weightless, high up in the cobalt blue vaults of the sky, resting on the face of the wind. The bird inside me must be a swift. Or wish it were.

Suddenly the semipalmated plovers startle, then lift, swirling off in one smooth oscillation. They bank out over the water, stream up over the horizon, then arch backward in a long, graceful curve, as if they were being sculpted by the wind. They return as abruptly as they left, falling out of the sky like drops of rain. I marvel at the simplicity of this design.

The birds appear to be orchestrated by a single voice, a pure infallible motivation.

Why why why, I wonder, do we have so much trouble figuring out what we are supposed to be doing? Why the endless choices every day: where and when and with whom to eat, to play, to sleep, to work, to procreate, to pray or not to pray?

I wonder if the birds have as clear a script for dying as they do for living. Or if they just fall one by one by one into the sea. Plip. Plip. Plup. Like us.

"What's the scoop, bird?" I say out loud to a chunky little ruddy turnstone, flipping pebbles at the tide line near my feet. He takes off like a bullet.

The onshore breeze that was freshening when I crossed from the pond to the barrier beach has died down. The sand is cool. How long have I been asleep? Gulls are crying. Through sandy slits I see an older couple walking by, both wearing white T-shirts and crisp khaki shorts. Their tidy presence makes me see myself as I have been for the past two hours, a middle-aged woman lying in the sand, out cold, mouth open probably, drooling probably. Now sitting upright, I begin brushing the sand from my face, my hands, my sweater. I study the gulls. They are hard to identify, so many phases, sizes. One is seeking my company. By way of little hops, two at a time, he has crept up to within ten feet. I take in every detail: blind white, chalk white, jet. Black on white. Gray like a mole. Gray like the sky before it snows.

He laughs.

I laugh.

He laughs.

I know he is thinking about the contents of my backpack. He knows I know. This does not change things.

The ebbing light tells me it is time to get going. I want to move down to the southern end of Chesapeake Bay before it gets dark. If I find a nice place to camp, I'll spend another day with the birds and the sky and the sea before I turn the bus to the west.

The three moderately sized RVs ahead of me have their right-turn indicators on. I flick mine on too, having seen a large sign saying FAMILY CAMPGROUND a couple of miles back. In truth, I have been following them for the past half hour. Last night made me feel a bit shaky, less sure of myself, so I don't want to repeat it. I am ready for this populated, well-organized campground by the bay.

My campsite is a grassy area beside the water. The sunset is wide: gold, pink, and green light-forms move upon the glassy water. Because my bus does not need electrical hookups, I am parked away from the others alone, but comfortably under the broad wing of the flock.

During the night I sleep smoothly, waking now and then on purpose to locate myself among the migrating constellations. Orion and the Pleiades, pulled up by Taurus, work their way forward in time. I dream about my mother. Wearing a crisp green-and-white dress, she stands near the entrance of a crowded room, as if she were about to leave. I am, as always, caught short by her physical beauty. Her stately carriage, high cheekbones, full red mouth. Then, realizing joyfully that she is still alive, I begin working my way toward her through the crowd. But she stops me with her eyes. I slow down, come to a halt in the middle of the rustling room. She is gazing at me alone. Her jeweled eyes are steady, opaque, like beads of lapis lazuli.

8

The Rapture and the Fear

When I finally got up the nerve to call Ben last night, he seemed as relieved as I was that the five years of silence between us was over. We made a plan to meet for lunch somewhere in Virginia tomorrow. I am to call him after I clear the city of Richmond. After that, I will begin the long haul to the Cheyenne Bottoms marsh in central Kansas, so today is designated rest day. A time to hang out with the other migrants in the sun.

I set up my chair just a few feet away from the lapping brim of the bay. High tide. The water eases its body ashore, crimping slightly around tough spikes of marsh grass. I plan to stay put today. Watch the tide flood, slack off, seep back in. I like the pace. And the idea of receiving one whole day, just as it is.

Releasing the two straps that connect the seat and backrest of my Crazy Creek chair, I lie down on my back. The September sun is bone-warming rather than hot. Rising thermals gyre silently over sun-soaked fields. I watch them strike the frigid currents arcing down from the north. Splashes of ice crystals mark each impact point. These intermingle and shred, then regroup again and then again until they grow smooth and white and pliant like kneaded dough. My mind soars up through the lace of nascent clouds, past deeper shoals of stratus, accelerating steadily as the molecules spread apart, until it reaches the deepest pools of sky, the place where mares' tails flick and trail.

What is it about the sky, about flight, that has so much to do with me?

The first time I thought about flying through the sky without an airplane around me, I was painting the interior of a large solitary house in the hills of Connecticut. It was 1961. Just home from a harebrained trip to Mexico with three other ski bums, I was very much at loose ends. So was my family.

I had been driven out of my parents' house by the menacing tick of the grandfather clock in the upstairs hallway, by the way it exaggerated the stillness in the house. Especially in the early afternoon, after cocktails and lunch were over and my parents napped like the dead on their beds.

The place I had been hired to paint had once been quite grand. Now it nodded like an ancient aunt in her chair by the window. The formal swimming pool was half filled with tannic sludge, and the remains of the perennial gardens were ruled by bold grasses tossing saucy purple tassels.

I had trouble with the afternoons there too. The long, silent hours of painting would begin pooling up around two o'clock. Some days I thought I would go crazy if I had to address one more window, if I had to think the same thought one more time. A week was all it took to wring out my usual fantasies. Then, out of my silent mind came elegant, clean images of flight.

The day after I finished the ground floor and moved my

supplies upstairs, I borrowed a car from my parents, drove two hours north, and threw my paint-speckled body out the door of an airplane. The next week I went back and did it again. And the next.

After that I had plenty to think about as I sanded until smooth the crusty layers of chipped paint around the windowpanes. Sometimes the thought of falling through the sky would make me so dazed with rapture that I would have to put down my brush and go outside to dream up into the deep blue eye overhead.

But the fear was always present too, coiled up inside. It would strike without warning, icing my heart, causing my rip cord to get stuck, my parachute to collapse, the ground to rush up like an oncoming freight train. At those times I would vow unequivocally, once and for all, never to jump out of an airplane again.

For a long time these forces were equal. I never knew whether or not I would jump again until I actually felt the slap of the slipstream beside the plane. Then one day, at the end of that summer, I made a jump that distilled my fear to the point of such purity, such intentionality, that I ceased to be afraid of the sky.

Colin and Will, two instructors at the skydiving center, and I had been watching a brooding mass of dark clouds northwest of the airport for more than an hour, hoping it would either come or go so we could get in a final jump that day.

Around five o'clock, Colin walked out to the loading area, took one last look at the inert storm, and began strapping a parachute onto his last student of the day, a first-time jumper by the name of Jim. "I don't think it's going to do anything after all," he said, yanking hard on Jim's leg straps. "If we hustle we should get a pretty high one in."

I had a lot of confidence in Colin. He was a well-seasoned

jumper and very competent. Still, when I hefted my chute over my shoulders and began snugging up the thick straps, a fresh embolus of fear broke open in my stomach. I watched Colin check the pins of the static line that would open Jim's chute automatically. His face was composed, shoulders relaxed. All business.

"I hope Colin knows what he's doing," I muttered to Will. We were walking out to the waiting jump plane.

"No problem," he replied, grinning crookedly as he cinched up the chin strap of his helmet. "We'll watch it as we climb. If it starts moving in, we'll jump from a lower altitude. But I think we can get a twenty-second free fall in, at the least."

The plan was to drop Jim off first, at 2,500 feet, and then climb up as high as the conditions would permit.

Watching Jim drop away from the door, mouth agape, eyes round as doughnuts, I noted that the cloud looked a lot closer, but Colin signaled to Dan, the pilot, to climb higher. I sat back in my seat, reminding myself that I was always scared before jumping, not to worry about it.

When we got to about 5,000 feet, Dan leveled off abruptly and cranked the plane around onto a jump run. He turned around in his seat and I saw that his face was ashen. "You've got to go. The storm is moving in fast."

We looked out the door and saw Jim's orange-and-white-striped canopy passing over the airport like a lost balloon. All the trees were bent in the same direction, the silver side of their leaves schooling like bait fish.

"He should have landed by now," I yelled to Colin.

"Jesus," he mouthed. He leaned farther out the door. Then he yelled up to Dan, "We're going to stay with you!"

"You can't! You have to go," Dan shouted in a strained voice. "I can't land back there, and I'm not sure I have enough gas to get me to another airport. It's safer to jump."

"We gotta go," Colin yelled as he moved back from the doorway to let us pass. "Get out! Now!"

Will dove through the door first. I broke out right after him, so close I flinched as the slipstream whipped his heels away from my face.

When I finally arched my back and spread out my arms and legs, the world below me came into sharp focus. Will was falling directly below me, his salmon-colored jumpsuit rippling around his body like an aura. Then the leading edge of the storm snatched him away. I checked the altimeter mounted on my reserve chute: 4,000 feet. Fragments of cloud began licking at me, and the green forest below flicked on and off like slides in a projector. Then the great cloud sucked me inside. I looked at my altimeter again. The needle was resting at 3,500 feet. Resting! Panic palsied through me.

That can't be, I thought, frantically tapping on the glass. *I'm falling!* But the little white pointer did not budge. Then I noticed a ghostly flower creeping up through the dim cloud, heading toward me. It was Jim, pendulating slowly under his canopy. He passed in eerie silence, disappearing over my head. I thought I was hallucinating. Just then my altimeter began to edge down again. But I didn't trust it. Nothing made sense. I grappled for my rip cord and yanked hard. My canopy paid out like a snake just as I broke out of the bottom of the cloud.

I was completely disoriented. All I could see was unbroken forest and a couple of unfamiliar lakes up ahead. I pulled my right toggle and spun the chute around so that I faced into the wind. The airport, about a quarter of a mile behind me, was sliding away fast. I felt like a man overboard, watching his ship sail away. Rotating around, I searched desperately for something solid, something for my mind to grab on to.

I spotted Will's yellow parachute first as it seesawed into

view about 500 feet away at the same altitude. His body was nearly parallel to the horizon at the top of each oscillation. Colin's bright red canopy stood out against the trees far below as it barreled along at fifty miles an hour, or more. Finally I located Jim's orange-and-white canopy floating far above me, fragile as an eggshell against the roiling lip of the storm.

I checked my altimeter. It was going up.

"Oh shit," I yelled in desperation. "How am I going to get down?" I remembered a harrowing book we had all read that summer, about a jet pilot, who, after ejection, had been sucked up into a thunderstorm. Up to 30,000 feet, where he would have died had he not had an exposure suit on. I saw the newspaper clippings of my death. "Oh no, I'm sorry," I wailed, remembering that I had not yet told my parents I had taken up skydiving.

Just then a thick bolt of lightning arched its back right next to me. My hair ends stretched out toward it. Then a mind-numbing crack of thunder split and peeled me clean. I felt utterly naked, like a shell, or a stone, like an embryo bobbing on a thread.

My orange-and-white parachute looked like a tiny flower against the dark face of the storm. Chaste with terror, I watched the forward lip buckle and pop as I rose and fell. It seemed impossible that something so fragile, so oddly beautiful, could be all that there was between my life and my death. It dissolved and bloomed with each shuddering crack.

I knew that the updraft of the rolling cloud at the front of the storm was preventing me from descending, but I didn't know what to do about it. Then I saw Colin's red parachute collapse in midair. I gasped. Hit by lightning! But the chute popped open again. Then it collapsed again. *Slipping!* I thought, remembering a procedure I had read about that was used by military jumpers during the Second World War to control their descents. I reached up and began to pull gingerly on one of my risers, afraid I might collapse the whole thing and drop like a stone to the ground. Nothing happened. I steeled myself and tried again, slowly adding all 110 pounds. The front lip of my chute started to curl and I felt a violent shaking. Then half the canopy caved in and I dropped like an elevator. Alarmed, I let go of the riser and the chute snapped back open. Colin looked a lot closer. It had worked. The horizon was actually rising. I looked around to get my bearings.

That was when I saw the lake dilating like a black pupil before me. *I don't believe this*, I thought. *Now I'm going to drown!* The only thing I could remember about water landings was that you were supposed to jump out of the harness the moment your toes hit the water. Otherwise, you could get tangled up in the lines and drown or be dragged across the lake facedown.

"God, please please please," I heard myself praying, as I unhooked one side of the reserve parachute lying across my lap and let it dangle down to the side. Then I sat back deeply in the harness until I was firmly cradled by the leg straps. I carefully unsnapped the D rings on the top of each groin, trying not to move lest I lose my balance and fall out. "GoddearGoddearGod," I intoned as I watched the lake accelerating toward me. I released my chest strap last, when I was about fifty feet off the water, and scooched my hips forward a bit to get ready to jump. Then, miraculously, the elevator zoomed upward again and I bounded up, clearing the trees at the far side of the lake by a hundred feet.

Quickly rebuckling my harness, I realized for the first time how fast I was moving over the ground. Even though I knew I could be dragged to death when I hit, I was desperate to reconnect with the earth any way I could.

The forest below me appeared to be seamless. Then I

noticed a logging road running to the east and steered for it. I was surprised at how quiet my body felt, as if the finality of what was about to happen had insulated me from the violence of the storm. The swinging tops of the evergreens looked soft and inviting. At about fifty feet, I turned around so I would go in back-first. I curled up into a fetal position, protected my head and neck with my arms, and then crashed into the treetops, careening grotesquely from tree to tree until my parachute snagged firmly on a branch. Then I plummeted like deadweight down through the limbs, a few at a time, until something caught hold again, and I bumped to a halt just a few feet from the ground. I didn't dare move. It was hard to believe that I was actually down. Alive.

A stalk of lightning slammed into the ground nearby and deftly jolted me back into the reality of my situation. I quickly unbuckled my harness and slipped to the ground. Another loud tick. Another crash, this one even louder. Then the rain came all at once, blinding me as I worked the parachute free from the tree. I stuffed it into its pack and began to run in the direction of the road, my body crouched low, my helmeted head parting the branches.

I heard a shout. Then another. "Here I am," I screamed into the wind. "Here! Here!" I stumbled toward the voice, until finally I made out a dim form running toward me. "Over here!" he cried out. And then as the swirling black raincoat approached me, "Are you all right? I heard the plane circling and I saw you go in. Come with me. Come!"

Bending low, I took off after him toward a shack in the distance. The wind, catching loose panels of my hastily packed chute, sailed me back and forth across the road.

When I entered the small shack, I had no idea where I was. It appeared to be a woodworking shop of some kind. My rescuer, a man in his midforties, with dark hair plastered against his head, pointed to a phone on the wall and said, "You probably want to use that." The storm was deafening. I called the airport and could barely hear the manager's voice saying, "Hello. Hello!"

"Walt. It's me, Anne. I'm safe!"

"Oh thank—"

Just then a bolt of lightning hit the shack. I rose like Peter Pan, flew across the room, and slammed hard into the back wall.

The next thing I knew, I was sitting on the floor, my legs splayed, stupefied. The woodworker ran toward me, shouting above the storm, "Holy Mother! You've been hit by lightning!"

I reached up and felt my head, my ears and eyes and cheeks, my neck. "I'm okay," I said cautiously.

"Stay where you are," he said firmly. "I'm going to get my truck. I'll get you out of here."

"I can come with you," I said, getting up slowly, checking each limb as I rose.

When he reached out his hand to help me up, he noticed my jump boots with their three-inch rubber soles. "Those probably saved your life right now," he said, whistling softly. "Boy, are you lucky!"

The hero of the day turned out to be the pilot. Even though he was dangerously low on gas, he chose to circle over us until each one of us had landed safely so that he could radio our positions back to the airport. The woodworker and I had barely reached the main road when we met a rescue truck in the back of which sat Colin and Will, both grinning broadly, and a dazed and drenched Jim, garlanded with leaves and pine needles and bits of twigs, his fogged-up glasses resting at a strange angle on his nose. That was the last we ever saw of him.

*   *   *

I brush sand off my arms and legs and reconstruct my chair. The coffee smells strong and sweet as I fill up my mug. We are such bewildering creatures, I muse, settling back into the embrace of the chair. How to explain this terrifying desire we all share to be lifted up and swept away by some giant force, to travel absolutely blind? We create gods for this purpose, form governments, go to the Sistine Chapel, the Met. And then we spend the rest of our time fighting to the death to maintain control over our lives, over time, over others. All this so we will not have to acknowledge what Mother Nature is actually doing: sweeping us right along in her massive arms like a great thunderstorm. What are our choices really?

Three sharp cries, very close. A dark wedge of greater yellowlegs pivots just above the horizon, cutting a bold furrow in the still morning air. The cries continue toward me. Help help there there here. Here! There is no gray in their speech. No excess.

I strain for language now as I sit by the water, searching its lacquered surfaces for a word that is wholly elemental. A bird word. A singularity out of which all life flows and flows.

9

The White Rabbit

The shock of Ben's disappearance five years ago was underscored by an unsettling irony. Ben loved surprise appearances. They were his specialty. He used to manifest like a rabbit out of a hat in the damnedest places, loving the jolt, the absurdity.

"Howdeedo," he'd croon, strolling into the old Hotel Crystal in Kathmandu, or stepping out of his fire-engine red airplane at some godforsaken airport where I was in hiding or in transit. One time, he showed up at Embry-Riddle Aeronautical University in Daytona Beach, where I was finishing up my flight instructor's license. His timing was perfect. "Howdeedo," he had warbled as I was tying down the airplane I had just been flying.

"Get in," I had replied briskly, motioning toward the passenger's seat. I remember the way he fumbled nervously with his seat belt. Up until then, he had always done the flying when we went up together. But I was too excited to be self-conscious about this "first," because I had just stumbled onto something that I knew was going to knock his socks off.

They were still there, the long dark ribbon of migrating

manta rays I had spotted just a few miles off the coast of Florida. I pulled back on the power, cranked on the flaps, and pressed the nose down below the horizon. We floated down in silence, arcing gently to the south until we were positioned right over a huge grizzled creature with a wingspan nearly matching ours. He was flying south in the warm waters of the Gulf Stream, a prehistoric bird, pulsing slowly, with remora fish streaming like rockweed from his hoary back. Neither of us spoke a word while we were with the rays, or on the flight back to the mainland; in fact, we never referred to the event again.

But that has been the story of our relationship for the past thirty years, really. The carefully edited version of reality—the mute rapture.

Today, however, I am really nervous about seeing him. A year ago I knew he was dead. No one had heard from him for four years and eleven months. And there was an enigmatic vision that kept manifesting itself at random moments . . . while I was jogging around the reservoir on Avon Mountain or looking out our kitchen window into the woods beyond. I would see him lying on his side on the ground, absolutely still, his head resting on his outstretched right arm, his alarmingly blue eyes gazing off in the distance, dried leaves lifting and drifting around him. For a couple of years I interpreted this to mean he was still alive. But as time passed, I became less sure. In my mind, the light behind his eyes began to dim.

I always thought we were on the same trip, Ben. For thirty years . . . no, more than that . . . I believed that our lives were linked in some subtle, vital way, the way planets are linked or wild geese flying in a skein. Where you were in time and space told me where I was. Until the day you left without a word. Then you were gone. Just gone.

"Are you okay?" Ben asks in a concerned voice as we settle into our seats inside the small roadside café in Powhatan, Virginia. "I couldn't tell from your phone call."

Words throng in my throat, but I cannot speak.

The man across the table is not Ben!

I knock this thought down quickly. *Settle down. This is not a ghost. It's Ben. Alive.*

"I mean, this isn't some trip into the sunset, is it?" he continues, noting my discomfort.

"Oh no. No!" I reassure him. Then I add with a reproving smile, "You're a fine one to ask that."

One side of his mouth tweaks up just a hair. He gives me a feigned salute and shifts sideways in his chair so that he can cross his long legs. The shoulders under his striped polo shirt relax. His full head of hair is now highlighted by whorls of gray. When his seriously blue eyes meet mine, I brace myself for what is coming.

He chooses his words precisely. "I usually ask people when I first meet them again if they have any questions they would like to ask me."

I recoil. A mutual friend, who had already reconnected with him, had told me this was his stock opener. I had been holding out for something different.

How can he just sit there, acting as if he had never died. As if it doesn't matter that we mourned him.

I take a swig of the cloudy water the waitress has set down before me, trying to tamp down my disappointment. I have been rehearsing this moment ever since I'd heard of that awful January day when he sat down at his desk and wrote a check for his oldest child's last semester in college and then a detailed letter to his wife, Julia, and the two boys telling them how proud of them he was, how much he loved them, why he had to leave them, how to proceed with what little was left of his fallen empire, and finally, that he would find them again, one day.

His family never stopped looking for him. They hired detectives, interviewed everyone he ever knew, contacted foreign embassies. Finally, after nearly five years had passed, they agreed to tell their story on a popular television series called *Unsolved Mysteries*. The day after the program aired, ten people called from a small town in Montana and said, "He's here." That was ten months ago.

After a long pause, I return his opening gambit. "I'm sure I do have questions, but I can't think of any right now." This is a blatant lie, but I don't like the way he is holding on to the reins of the conversation.

We sit there for a while. He is watching me the way he always does . . . to see what I will do. And I am watching him. This is what we have always done. In fact, right now we are behaving just as we have ever since we were freshmen in college. Spare with words. Closely tuned in to each other's gestures, expressions, on what was not being said. We both come by this aptitude honestly, having grown up in homes where subtext was the primary language.

When we met on spring break in 1959, we were both pretty wild. Not in the way of drugs or sex; it was more subtle, like the wildness of caged birds, or an unspoken dare. Every time we got together, we almost ran away. That was the dare, I think. To just walk out of our dormitories or homes, out of the scripts that were already written for us, and keep going. This fired us up in marvelous ways, even though we never would have done it because of our ties to our families. So we fled to the woods, to the ocean floor, up into the mountains and the sky . . . to places that were new and immaculate and immediate, where everything was possible. We found chanterelles the color of sunset pushing through loamy forest floors, we studied lightning and clouds and meteor showers, we fantasized about flying to Peru so we could witness the blinding flash of green that cauterizes the horizon at sunset when the sun slides into the sea.

We never talked about the fact that both our families were struggling with sad, life-altering problems at that time, or how those circumstances were affecting us. The time we spent in each other's households obviated any need for words.

When there are no words, all acts become critical. I remember the first time he came to see me at my parents' summer place in Rhode Island. After a late-night walk on the beach, Ben had dropped me off at our cottage and headed back to his college. While I was getting ready for bed, I sensed that he would be coming back, that he had something he wanted to tell me. I put on my bathrobe and crept downstairs, careful not to wake the household. I did not turn on any lights, just sat in the wicker chair facing the front door, waiting for the lights of his car to bend back into the driveway.

When he arrived at the door, his face looked very pale in the weak moonlight. He stood silently on the doorstep, looking at me through the screen door. I waved him in, but he shook his head. He had hit a seagull as he was driving out the shore road, he said. When he stopped to pick it up, it had looked him directly in the eye, and then it had died in his hands. Holding them out before him, he said he could still feel the warmth of the bird in his palms. Then he turned around and drove away.

When we were in our twenties, people assumed we were lovers because we seemed so close. But it wasn't true. In those days, I gravitated toward inappropriate men only, preludes to my first husband who kept my parents in a state of breathlessness for years. Still, on the night he told me that he was getting married, I was overwhelmed by loneliness. I cried and cried. Even though I was truly happy for him—Julia was a wonderful, strong woman—even though I was, at that moment, packing up my life possessions to move to Florida to marry Zeus and his thunderbolts. By then, the gap between the bold and breezy self I presented to my family and friends and the increasingly isolated one I kept hidden from them had grown too large for words. Ben was, by virtue of our uncanny twinning, the only person who knew about the one I had quarantined inside of me. In fact, he was the only way I could connect with that self. Being with him was like watching myself in a distant mirror. The image frightened and fascinated me.

And it still does, I have to admit. Especially now, when I am trying to figure out where he has been, and where I'm headed.

Suddenly Ben looks sad. Or tired. I can see how hard this must be for him, this reclaiming of friendships, one by one. All those words he has to serve up. I feel guilty for wanting something more from him right now. Part of me wants to say let's bracket this and go on the way we were, but I know this is impossible; we are no longer who we were.

He begins. "I know everybody thinks I was depressed. It's not true. I was in big financial trouble, with too many things coming due. When the bottom dropped out of the real estate market, I just couldn't keep all the oranges up in the air; they were coming down all over the place. It was a nightmare."

"But Julia! What about Julia? And Pete and Sam."

"I thought it would be worse for them if I hung around. The disgrace. They didn't know about any of this. No one did. I failed them. That was all there was to it. There was no way to reverse it."

Once again I regret our last conversation two weeks before he disappeared. He had called the day after David and I returned from a three-month sabbatical in Nepal. I had no idea that he was in the midst of a crisis. The phone had rung at the wrong moment: while I was hurrying to get David, who was in terrible pain from a badly shattered ankle, dressed to go into the hospital for surgery.

I remember two things about the phone call. When I asked

him how his business was doing, he said, "Terrible." But he said it casually, like a joke. Because we were already running late, I chose not to question him further. The other thing I remember was that I told him I would call him back in a couple of days. Which I did not do. With David in the hospital, and everyone coming for Christmas, three weeks slipped by. Then during the first week in January came the terrible phone call telling me that he had vanished off the map.

"Did you have a plan?" I ask softly.

"Yes and no. But I tried not to think too far ahead. One day was hard enough to get through. I knew I would try to find them again someday. That's all."

All at once, I see his sorrow. Long, ignoble, unyielding. And for the first time I feel the profound sense of failure that made him give up everything he loved in life.

I change tacks. "The last sign of you was a credit card receipt from a store in Chicago. We guessed you were traveling west by train."

"Toothbrush. Two shirts, underwear, socks, a bag to put them in. I had bought a ticket to Seattle."

"I heard you were on the streets there for quite a while."

"I tried to find work there. Anything. Fast food. Gas station. No one would hire me. Every time I gave someone my social security number they would disappear into a back room, then come back and say, 'Sorry, we don't have anything for you.'"

I imagined him standing in an an urban gas station: fifty-six years old, white Brooks Brothers shirt, blue blazer, gray trousers probably—he had visited his mother in New York City the day he took off—carrying his worldly possessions with him: a small duffel bag and his laptop. Not a great candidate for pumping gas, I guess.

"I still don't know what was wrong with me," he says simply as if reading my thoughts. "It was very strange."

They probably thought you were crazy, I don't say.

He pauses while the waitress pours our coffee. "When my money was nearly gone, I moved into an alley behind the fleabag hotel where I had been staying. It wasn't too bad. I would sleep with my back against the wall, my knees drawn up, hiding my laptop against my chest."

You were crazy, I don't say. *This doesn't happen to people like us.*

He goes on to tell me how he had landed in Montana, using the last of his money for a bus ticket, how he had begun to teach in a computer school while living in the bus station. How he had managed to organize a skeletal existence, a holding pattern, so to speak.

"What did you think about during that time?" I ask incredulously.

"I tried not to think. Every day was a series of challenges. The four-mile walk to the computer school. Scrounging for students—I had to build up a client base from scratch. It was very hard at first because I got paid by the student hour. I had to figure out how to eat, how to sleep at the bus station without getting in trouble, how to stay clean. It took a long time for me to accumulate enough money for the first and last months' rent on a place to live. I eventually found an unfurnished apartment for a hundred dollars a month."

"Unfurnished," I repeat, trying to create a mental picture. "No bed, no pot, no pan?"—I pause, trying to piece something, anything, together—"No blanket? No pillow?"

"No nuttin," he says lightly. But his eyes are solemn. "Sundays and holidays were the worst. The school wouldn't let me work, and I didn't have anything else to do. On those days it was impossible to avoid thinking about my family, but when I did, it made me nearly crazy."

I thought of the long empty days when I was on the road in my twenties, how I would stretch everything out. Tooth-brushing. Nail clipping. But he had a phone call he could have made. "I can't believe you didn't call them."

"I came close a lot of times. But what did I have to offer them at that point? I knew I would try to find them again some day. When I got back on my feet. That's as far as my mind could go. The funny thing was that I was actually making it. Very slowly. My student load was growing. I was able to buy a mountain bike for transportation to work and recreation on the weekends. When my family found me, I had saved almost enough money to buy a motor scooter. That would have changed my life a lot."

I finish my coffee soberly, trying to measure the weight of this story. It feels like a meteorite, composed of elements my mind cannot conceive of. I try to imagine his reunion with Julia and the boys. What did they say to each other? I have no idea what to say to him.

Walking out to the parking lot, I realize I am not ready to say good-bye. The place where he has been that I have not is still holding us apart. He senses this and raises the hatchback of his car so we can sit for a few more minutes in the sun. I cast around for common ground, something that will reconnect us. I tell him about my trip. He seems to understand what I am trying to do, and why. When we get on to the subject of migration, I prod his memory.

"Do you remember the manta rays we saw migrating down the coast of Florida?" I ask, drawing up my knees and crossing my ankles.

His face brightens into a big grin. "That was really something, wasn't it?"

"That was the first time you ever flew with me," I remind him. "You were a basket case!"

"For good reasons," he teases. "I'd driven with you in a car."

We sit quietly for a minute or two, enjoying the comfort of

shared history. And too, the fact that we have actually made it through this first encounter.

"Do you want to spend the night at our place?" Ben asks finally. "We have plenty of room now Pete's back at school. Just Julia and me now and a lot of dogs."

"Thanks. No. I've got a long way to go. The waterfowl migration is already in full swing in Kansas."

We walk over to my car and face each other awkwardly.

Ben looks off into the woods beyond the parking lot. "You were the only one who called me a shit after I got back . . . in your letter. Do you still feel that way?"

"I think I just wanted you to know how much it hurt. Besides," I add with an apologetic shrug, "somebody had to say it."

"So, how does this chapter end?"

"I dunno . . . One thing I'm sure of now is that I didn't make it all up. That's been worrying me."

"Make all what up?"

"You. Who you were in my life."

He drops his gaze and shifts his weight back and forth. "I always thought our relationship was absolutely unique." He turns his head back toward the woods. "That it was a place apart from ordinary life."

"We always made it through the looking glass . . . didn't we . . . when we were together?"

He laughs, then hesitates for a moment. "Does what I did change that now?"

"I don't know. But we're standing here in Virginia, of all places. Talking about it."

"That's a lot," he says, a slow grin spreading.

"It's a start," I confirm as I stretch up on my tiptoes to kiss him on the cheek.

10

Bears in the Woods

I hate the way I feel right now: whiny, lily-livered, unsure of myself. I was stupid to let myself get blown off course this afternoon the way I did. The mountains of West Virginia looked so glorious in the mirror-bright autumn light, so virginal; I just couldn't turn my back on the prospect of a remote clearing in the woods, a snapping twig fire, of sleeping by it on the ground, even though I had made up my mind that I was going to forgo that kind of thing on this trip. Yet to drive by these mountains at sixty miles an hour on the interstate because of a few nameless fears seemed the greater misdeed.

What got suppressed, however, was the fact that ever since my friend Lee was murdered in the woods, *in my home woods,* those fears have not been so nameless.

At least twenty years have passed since the afternoon she swung into my driveway, her kayak lashed to the top of her Volkswagen bug like a captured porpoise. "I need to get wet," she had announced. "Come on, we'll just go for a couple of hours." Light blue eyes, a long swinging rope of blond hair. In her midtwenties, Lee was as powerful as she was beautiful. I vacillated for a couple of irreversible moments as we stood outside in the early spring sunshine, then told her that I *had* to get my grades in that day, but would definitely go with her the next day.

She died thirty minutes later in the woods a few miles away, fighting the man who was trying to rape her and his knife with her feet as her boyfriend had taught her to do. I lost so much that day. My friend, my freedom.

But there was more to lose. When her murderer was captured two weeks later, the evening news showed a film clip of the police escorting him from his house into the waiting cruiser. To my eternal horror, I recognized the young man, his dark curly hair, his boyish face and baseball jacket. He had frightened me badly a few weeks before while I was hiking by myself along a cliffside trail on Avon Mountain. Stepping out from behind a clump of trees, he had fallen in step with me, saying in a cheerful voice, "Hi. Do you mind if I join you?" I had tensed immediately, even though he looked more like a college boy than a threat. Several rapes had been reported in a state park not far from there.

I didn't want him to know I was afraid of him, so I replied politely, "Sorry, I'm meeting my husband just ahead." Fortunately, I spotted a side trail a few feet in front of us. After we had both walked by it, I turned back toward it, saying, "Oops, that's my trail. Bye!" As soon as I was out of his sight, I broke into a full run, slipping and skidding as I tore down the steep path toward the parking lot about half a mile away. After a few seconds, I looked back. Through the leafless trees, I saw his dark form dropping down the trail behind me; he was closing in on me fast. White with adrenaline, I pushed my arms and legs until I could not feel them anymore, only the terrible scraping in my lungs.

Then I heard the sound of children's voices, rising up through the trees. A school group! Straggling up the path in clumps, teachers and parents and kids, stretching all the way back to the parking lot.

My heart is bounding now as the memory completes its rerun. I have tried so hard not to let those events change the way I feel about being alone in the woods; indeed I have gone about my life as always, but it has changed me in subtle ways because I know that such a thing *could* happen to me. Ever since Lee died, I have watched my back, whether I wanted to or not.

This afternoon my plan had been to get off the interstate a couple of hours before Charleston so that I could locate the main bridge over the New River. Then I figured I could explore the area in ever-widening circles until I found the campsite in my head. But when I stopped at a small grocery store to buy supplies for the night, my body alarm began to sound. The parking lot was filled with trucks, each one occupied by two motionless people. A fragile menace appeared to be holding everyone in place, everyone but me. As I crossed the parking lot and stepped up onto the wooden porch, I felt absurdly out of proportion with my environment, as if like Alice in Wonderland I had suddenly mushroomed up. Neither the man nor the woman behind the counter greeted me when I entered. They simply stared straight at me, their silence compact, aggressive. I awkwardly selected a bottle of grapefruit juice I did not really want and left quickly.

My exploration of the back roads near the deep gorge confirmed the hostility I had sensed in the store. And because it was midweek and off season, I was the only stranger around. At every pullout, I encountered silent men in parked trucks. They would take careful aim with their eyes and then stare at me evenly, making it clear that I had entered their space and that they were the ones who set the rules there. I avoided their eyes, refusing to complete the circuitry while I wheeled the bus around, conscious of the fact that a fifty-some-odd-year-old woman with shoulder-length hair, wearing a blue Patagonia jacket with a Tibetan Buddhist *dorge* embroidered on the back, traveling alone in a vintage camper with Connecticut plates and a turkey feather dangling from the rearview mirror might qualify as fair game.

One of these confrontations stopped my heart cold. Trying to get back to the main road and out of there, I mistakenly chose a dead-end road. A copper-colored pickup was parked in the center of the turnaround. In it sat two men, watching me approach. The stillness of their bodies made it clear that I would have to back up and maneuver the bus around in the small area left at the neck of the circle. As I was backing up, I heard the truck fire up. When I turned my head to shift into first, I saw it edge forward slightly until it just blocked my way. "Shit. I've had it," I hissed, slamming the gearstick back into reverse. But I had no place to back into except the woods. They let me sit there and feel the situation for an interminable moment, until I finally looked up at them. Then, with a sarcastic smile on his face, the driver wagged his head like I was the stupidest creature alive, backed up, and let me flee.

They were just playing with me, I told myself as I drove back to the main bridge. No big deal. Black bears will do that, feign a charge just to let you know who's who. The problem is my body reacts the same way to all scenarios.

The visitors' center by the gorge yielded a brochure that listed a number of camping areas. One sounded rather promising, "quiet wooded sites, lovely views." So I headed off to the east. Forty long minutes passed before the small sign for River Road appeared on my left. Relieved, I made a sharp turn as directed, then stopped abruptly. There, right beside the four-lane highway, three despondent pull-trailers loitered in a weedy patch surrounded by barbed wire. Pulling over, I reached for the guidebook, assuming I had made a mistake. But then I spotted the hand-painted sign, pinned to a tree like a misplaced tail on the donkey. On it were the words nEW rIVEr SEnic camPiNg.

"Why am I doing this?" I wailed as I spun the bus around one more time. The question hung in the air like a scarlet banner as I negotiated my way back to the interstate.

I am still wondering as the city of Charleston slips behind me. The question of fear is a door I don't like to open because it has so much to do with how I've lived my life. But after this afternoon's ignominious rout, I realize that my fears, both real and imagined, could ruin this trip for me . . . if I continue to disown them.

I have to remember that it's normal to feel fear in certain situations, and this afternoon was probably one of them. The problem is that in the world of humans—and other predators—fear is a sign of weakness. "Never show a bear that you are afraid," a naturalist once told me. "If you do, they will identify you as prey."

But why is fearlessness so important to me? What am I trying to prove?

I am surprised how defiant these two questions make me feel. It probably has to do with the fact that I grew up at a time where boys got preferential treatment at home, at school, in sports. I knew this the way I knew my name. I saw the way my mother deferred to my father, my grandmother to my grandfather, and the way they all, in subtle ways, deferred to their sons. And while I adored the males in my family, I realized I was being treated differently and I didn't like it.

My brother Jimmy and his friends spent a good part of their childhoods trying to scare the hell out of my girlfriends and me. They threatened us with poison sticks, tied us to trees, told us hideous stories about jibbering psychos rampaging in our neighborhood. At times, however, they invited us to test their manhood with them . . . on the condition that we go first. And so Eleanor and Barbara and I leapt off the garage roof with bedspread parachutes, inched our way out onto the transparent ice of the skating pond. In July at the shore, Juliette and I ignited their mail-order cherry bombs, dropped them into empty paint cans, and hurled them off the dock. The message was as clear as the black ice we ventured out on: if you can overcome your fear, you can do anything. Everything!

In spite of the gender inequities, there are no sour grapes attached to these memories of my childhood. My brother and his overstimulated little friends taught me that life could be absolutely thrilling. That my life was not going to be like my mother's and my grandmother's as long as I was able to deal with my fears. When I think of racing home after dark from Eleanor's house with all those maniacs hiding in the hedges, I remember feeling wild and strong, like a mustang or a fighter pilot. The half-a-block trip would have been nothing without the maniacs, nothing at all.

That's the irony of it all, isn't it?

But then there is the story of Lee. The men in the woods today. The voices in my head saying, *What's the matter with you, anyway?* These are the voices of the people who ask me why David "lets" me take off by myself the way I do. The word makes me crazy. "What do you think he is," I want to snap back, "my keeper?" Instead, I shrug my shoulders and smile sheepishly, knowing that there are more complex questions being asked, to which I have no glib reply: *Why do you insist on doing this to him? Why do you have to be so independent?* Or sometimes: *Wow, how do you do it?* These are good questions. I ask them of myself every time I leave. There are some tempting answers available, all of them clichés, and sometimes out of fatigue or fear of losing what I so deeply want, I give in to them, displacing the truth like a careful breaststroker, keeping it just ahead of me, all the while moving forward.

The truth is that David worries a lot about me when I am away. And to make matters worse, he gets horridly lonely. The only thing I can say in behalf of my behavior is that the equilibrium of our marriage depends on a precise chemistry: my exuberance for flight balancing his fear of falling; his passion for form defining my shadows; his sudden jolts of blue-eyed laughter, clean as a kid's, inoculating me against the dark.

All of a sudden I miss him terribly. The way he steps toward me from the kitchen when I enter the house, enlivened, expectant. "Hi!" he calls out as if we haven't seen each other for days, reaching for my grocery bags and kissing me solidly. "David!" I reply, filling up once again with the wonder of finding this beautiful man in my house. Second marriages are like this. Having really blown it once, divorced people find it hard to believe the gods would give them another chance.

A large sign has just caught the edge of my sight. FAMILY CAMPING 15 MILES. Perfect. I'll call home from there. My longing for David swells like a bruise. So does my guilt. Sometimes I feel as if I will never come to grips with the price that women have to pay for freedom. Everything a woman owns as a wife and mother is also someone else's: her time, her energy, her emotions, her spirit. To take what she needs, she has to carve it right out of the center of family life. Dead center. Many would argue that this is true for men as well, but I don't agree. Men are supposed to "go for it." They are brought up that way.

I pull into the campground just as the light becomes lavender. Following instructions, I drive down a narrow dirt road until I reach an open swath cut from the great rolling forest that is West Virginia. The caretaker has directed me to this rather lovely but entirely empty field some distance from the main camping area, saying, "We usually put folks like you who don't need hookups out there in the boonies. You'll like it."

Unrestrained by parking slots or picnic tables, I pull into the center of the field and turn off the engine. I sit quietly for several minutes, listening to the humming woods, trying to determine where I am in relation to the line that separates solitude and isolation. Darkness descends rapidly, sealing off the field from the rest of the world. I feel the woods cinch in around me; the bears start to inch forward.

"No way!" I say to the bears as I turn over the engine and start backtracking to the main camping area. There I find a site surrounded by large trees, somewhat apart but also on the periphery of the knot of RVs that compose the communal hearth.

The evening is silky; under the shade trees around my campsite, the shadows collect into deep, featureless pools. After talking for a long time with David on the pay phone by the shower house, I pour a glass of white wine and take my time sautéing zucchini, red peppers, and portobello mushrooms to mix with the spinach fettuccine I bought back in Virginia.

When I am finally curled up under the reading light, I come across a discussion of *displacement activity* in my Audubon encyclopedia. This is a random kind of violence that occurs in animals when the normal path for a strong drive is thwarted, or when two strong drives occur simultaneously. For example, falcons are known to attack and kill passing birds when frightened by humans who have ventured too near their nests. That's how I felt today. Like a passing sparrow.

Then, out of curiosity, I look up *flocking*: "Some observers have compared it with hunger—a craving or sensation of discomfort arising from the absence of a physical requirement . . . social stimuli."

Okay, okay, I got it. I need to stay with the flock. No, I choose to stay with the flock. Period.

After I turn out the overhead lamp, I reopen the curtains. The red glow of a campfire signals from across the clearing. Near it, a kerosene lantern, probably hanging from a tree, burns a soft white hole in the night.

I fall asleep with the windows of my bus open wide, with fingers of cool night air tracing patterns on my forehead, my eyelids.

11

My Time as a Bird

The sky has been gaining ground all day, mile by mile by mile. Having just crossed the Wabash River, I now move out onto the great disk of Illinois. My body feels light and breezy, as if someone just snatched off my sombrero. In the distance, a huge cumulus cloud emotes silently. I recognize this cloud. It is an old friend. Every time I see it, I feel the same slap of joy, and the same pictures come tumbling slowly through my mind.

During my three years on the United States Sport Parachuting Team, I logged more than three hours of free fall. Mefall. One minute of this time, sixty seconds precisely, remains very near the surface of my mind. It happened while I was in training with the team at a skydiving center in Orange, Massachusetts.

Finished with our training for the day, my teammates and I were sitting around the loading area of the airport, loafing in the sun, watching the skydiving instructors from the local center suit up their students. A cold front had just passed through the night before; the sky, vibrating like the sea at noon, was punctuated by brilliant towers of cumulus clouds.

As the newest and least experienced member of the team, I was pleased when Joe, a veteran of several world competitions, sat down beside me; I had never really talked to him. Joe was a career army man, a classical sergeant: exacting, resolute, circumspect. Except for his huge sad eyes, and his lilting humor.

I pointed to a crisp white spire, floating above the airfield. "Isn't that just magnificent?"

"Sure is," he said quietly. There was a pause and then he turned to me, his melancholy eyes oddly electrified. "Have you ever punched a cloud before?"

Not sure of what he meant, I shrugged my shoulders. "I don't think so." Then, feeling like a hopeless neophyte, I added, "I guess I don't know what you mean."

He reached over, picked up my freshly packed parachute, and slid it over my shoulders. As he checked my rip cord pins, he said, "Let's go. I've got something to show you."

Belted into our seats in the darkness of the jump plane, Joe and I watched the jump master dispatch his students one by one. It had been a while since either of us had jumped just for the fun of it, and we were revved up. "Have you ever tumbled backward out of the plane?" I yelled at him over the drumming of the engine. "Just fallen out, like it was a mistake?"

"No I have not, little lady," he replied in his slow southern speech. A member of the Special Forces, Joe had been stationed in South Carolina for many years. He nodded a couple of times, grinning. "We could do that if you wish."

After the silhouette of the last jumper vanished from the wide, bright doorway, the pilot looked back at us for instructions. Joe made an upward spiraling motion with his forefinger, and the plane banked into a tight right turn. As we climbed out, I noticed that we were scaling the side of one of the billowing towers. Soft explosions of vapor and light bloomed beside us as we spun higher and higher.

By the time we reached 12,500 feet, the sky was empty, a singular brilliance. Joe moved into the doorway. "I want to spot this one if you don't mind." I nodded, happy to let someone else do it for a change. Working the intercom buttons that flash in the cockpit, he began directing the pilot to our exit point. When he hit the cut button, he motioned me to the door. Crouching low, I was getting ready to dive out of the plane when Joe took me by the shoulders and turned me around so that my back was to the door. "Close your eyes and fall out backward. Like it was a mistake. Like you said."

As I sit in the blue bus, writing out this story, I feel out of breath. I remember every detail. Every sensation. In my mind I tip over backward slowly, holding on to my knees. And then, as if released from a bow, I streak into the afternoon. When I open my eyes, the airplane is banking away, getting smaller, abandoning me. I roll into a back loop, closing my eyes again. Sky tumbling. Black white black white, I allow my body to spin deliriously out of control, until centrifugal force begins to whip me into a tight spin. Then I open my eyes, spread out my arms and legs, and arch my back to stabilize. Joe is lying about twenty feet above me, watching, a wide grin ruffling on his face. I spread my arms and legs out as wide as I can to slow my fall while he pulls his arms and legs in close to his body and drops down until we are lying on the same cushion of air, face-to-face, about four feet apart. We move together slowly, eyes locked, hands out in front of us, palming and fingering the slipstream, carefully closing the space between us. We clasp hands and kiss, goggles bumping, faces rippling. Even now, I can feel the soft pressure of his mouth.

When we break apart, Joe points downward, jabbing emphatically. Have we lost track of time? Is it the ground? I lower my eyes through the horizon. About 2,000 feet below me, a great white cloud is detonating silently. I see Joe pull his arms back like a ski jumper so that he can track toward its mounding central core. I do the same, guiding my trajectory by rounding my back and steering with cupped hands. I fly forward until I am centered perfectly, then flare out my arms and legs. Below me on the surface of the cloud, I see a dark spot unfold. "Dear God," I exhale forcefully, "that's me!"

I watch the tiny froglike creature grow for a few moments, and then everything starts accelerating, and I am barreling toward myself. Cloud rush. Instinctively, I pull my arms in, preparing to dive headfirst into the billow. An arrow. The dark point that is me races toward me. We collide in a stunning explosion. Without sound. Without impact.

The abrupt formlessness is disorienting. Gray wisps of vapor float upward; I cannot tell if I am falling or soaring. Flicking strips of light gently strobe my eyesight, and time begins to slow down, spread out, circle around me. This makes me anxious. I look for Joe, for the ground, something, anything that will let me know where I am—or what I am, for that matter.

That night, drinking beer with our teammates at the Inn at Orange, Joe and I signed off the jump in each other's logbooks, trying our best to stifle our ebullience. Earlier we had been firmly reprimanded by our coach, our team leader, and the airport manager because it is against federal aviation regulations to enter clouds without permission. But every time our eyes connected across the table, Joe and I would break into witless grins and roll our eyes like villains. It was fun to be in childlike collusion with this serious sergeant, this highly trained soldier, this man of few words.

Years later, when I was going through my old logbooks, I found a note from Joe. Written that night, it was hidden away on one of the empty pages in the back.

Little bird,
How you beguile
Tender tough,
Woman child.

As I reenter the world of Interstate 80 and its obedient streams of cars, parting and merging, ever flowing, I think of an image I came across last night while browsing through my Audubon encyclopedia. It was a line drawing of a pair of bald eagles tumbling through the air, talons very nearly touching. During their nuptial flight, the caption under it reveals, the male drops down from above and brushes the female gently on her back; then feet together, the two may go rolling over and over and over in the sky.

I can relate to that, I muse happily, shaking my head with wonder.

The clouds over Illinois are now rearing up into a giant tsunami. In the shadow of its curl, the world has grown hushed, expectant. I feel it too, the great suck of the engine powering the approaching front. Out here, there is no place to hide from the sky. Whether you hold fast, run like hell, or barrel right toward it, it's going to roll over you no matter what. I find this thought absolutely thrilling.

If I could choose one reality to live in, I would take this one any day over the comfortable little world I call my life, I say to myself, feeling quite cosmic and very smug for a moment or two. That is, until I realize that this choice has already been made for me and there is no safe little world . . . Anywhere.

12

Winging It in the Cosmos

St. Louis, Missouri. Awash in a stone-gray haze, the Great Gateway Arch takes shape gradually. I watch it pull in tight like a massive bow. Shaped more by sky than steel, its symmetry touches a geometry my body recognizes, and my spirit bows its head.

According to my road map, the interstate will curl to the right around the eastern side of the arch and then track off to the west. As I move toward it at sixty miles an hour, the rigid structure flexes its limbs, as if just waking up. Then it begins to twist and bend like a dancer. Now it is a Gothic arch, now a soaring pillar. Suddenly it pirouettes, making me laugh out loud. *Every moment is a new and perfect work of art!* I announce triumphantly. My part in this composition exhilarates me.

Beyond the city and its performing arch is the great airscape of the West. For those of us who spend our lives lurking around under the dark canopy of New England's forests, the West is like a bucket of cold water in the face. You don't know how much you need it until it hits you, and there you are: bright-eyed and bushy tailed, as my father used to say.

In a few hours I will cross over into Kansas. I am heading for a blank spot on the map, really. Number ten on a list of thirty-nine major staging posts for migrating birds on the planet Earth. Here are some of the others: Tierra del Fuego. Bals Fjord. Lake Chad. Ammassalik. No wonder I am pinking up, minute by minute.

For the first time in a long time, I am exactly where I want to be in time and space. The past lies on the other side of the Gateway Arch. The future enters with each breath. In this sliver of time, when my mind constructs reality and responds to it simultaneously, I know myself as I really am, an interstellar traveler, a shape-changing, irrepressible speck of cosmic debris.

And even though my mind will never stop trying to grab on to passing tree trunks and boulders, anything that might make the world seem more solid, it stores our true history carefully in the baton-pass of its cells. So when I wake up in the night at home as I sometimes do, facing that absolute wall of oblivion, feeling that icy shock of fear rip through my body, I can coax myself back to the reality of my atoms. Born in the blast of an exploding star, these particles belong to the universe and are no more me or mine than the wind rocking the tree outside the French doors of our bedroom in the moonlight. As the fear subsides, I turn to David, sleeping on his side facing away from me, slide my body full length along his, and then together we curl up, he taking my right hand and holding it fast over his heart. He always sighs happily, remembering me in his sleep, and then I let myself dissolve back into the night.

Two hundred and fifty miles to Kansas City, then Topeka, then Cheyenne Bottoms marsh. Now that I am truly in the West, I travel as the crow flies, hugging the curve of the earth. I feel as if I could do this all night. Maybe I will.

13

Winging It in Kansas

The massive cold front that has been bullying me all day has finally launched its attack. The wind is batting the bus around so much that it doesn't know whether to take off, or tip over, or do the tarantella. I can barely make out the signs for downtown Topeka through the frozen slog whacking back and forth on my windshield. I know I should have stopped earlier, but it looked so mean and cold out there. Now it is after nine, and I am in the middle of a maelstrom in a strange city. What was I thinking of?

The only signs of refuge I have been able to decipher are billboards for large chain motels. I hate these places more than I hate most things, but follow the signs anyway. What are my options? I comfort myself by envisioning the next morning, writing at a real table in my room for a few hours, my laptop battery recharging away.

Exhausted from fifteen hours of driving, I pay the $70 without flinching, in spite of the fact that the cavernous lobby contains a large chemical-wafting swimming pool. The home fire is definitely not a concept in this place. But when I enter my room, I lose it. The room has no exterior windows. Door closed, it is as tight as a submarine.

I grab my bags, march back to the elevator, troop across the lobby, and in a strained, unpleasant voice announce to a bored desk clerk that I cannot possibly sleep in that room. "I'll pay more," I tell her haughtily. "I don't care how much." She looks at me blankly, so I intone my words syllable by syllable, bulging out my eyes like a lunatic. "I *need* a *room* with a *window! Please!*" The clerk exchanges eye rolls with her coworker, then replies in an exasperatingly polite voice, "I'm sorry, ma'am, there *are* no rooms with windows."

"Ma'am," I mumble to myself as I retrace my steps to my room and shove my bags back through the door. I hate it when people call me ma'am.

Dinner is all that I have between me and my cell. Seated in the nearly empty dining room at a table for four, I order chicken-something-or-other sandwiched between two cold slabs of canned pineapple. After spending a lot of time chewing slowly while squinting at an old *New York Times Magazine* and pretending I don't know I am the only one left in the restaurant, I reluctantly return to my sarcophagus and turn on all the lights as well as the huge television that looms over my bed like a gargoyle. I never know what to watch on TV. I try a program about a cheetah ripping apart an impala, then one about cops pulverizing scumbag crooks in southern California. I end up reading most of the night, finishing E. Annie Proulx's compelling *Postcards* just before the clock indicates dawn.

Threading my way back to the interstate, I feel edgy, as if I have eaten too much chocolate. Maybe my reaction to the motel's architecture was exacerbated by the fact that I have been living outside for nearly a week. Besides, chain motels remind me of my first husband. He liked them, said he liked knowing what to expect when he was on vacation. Some holiday he was.

Denver got buried by eleven inches of snow last night, says the radio. And it is snowing ahead of me in central Kansas right now. To top it off, a wide swath of freezing rain fans out behind me. There is no way to escape from this day.

But I am going to Cheyenne Bottoms Wildlife Management Area today no matter what. When I called the headquarters near Great Bend earlier, the ranger told me the waterfowl migration was in full swing, but the birds would probably be hiding out in the cattails because of the storm. *Sounds fine to me*, I say to myself, *better than a chlorinated motel.*

In spite of my gravelly mood, I am excited to be getting back to the birds after two full days on the road. In their absence I have been telescoping in on whatever presents itself: spiders, afternoon clouds, conversations in restaurants. This can be pretty unsettling when, without meaning to, you tap into something unprotected, as I did this morning while watching an aging salesman with shoe-polish black hair swept up but not quite over his bald spot try to start up a conversation with a young waitress in the motel restaurant. The blunt force of his loneliness had, for a time, held all of us in the salmon-colored dining room hostage.

"Are you always this nice to everybody?" he had begun coyly, as she passed him a menu. Looking around the restaurant for eye contact, he got me before I could duck, winked conspiratorially, then turned back and addressed her in a much louder voice as she filled up his water glass.

"Wow, you're good. Are you always this good, sweetheart? I mean this grr-eat!" Hopeful, he had canvassed the room again, his hunger driving all of our eyes down this time, and it sent the waitress to a serving station across the room where she self-consciously restacked plates. With just two relatively benign questions, he had done something really quite amazing. The room had become as still as a convent. People were eating their eggs and bacon obediently, eyes on their plates, heads down. No one wanted to feel the weight of that loneliness; it was just too innocent to bear.

Big sky here in Kansas. Two horses stand in the rain on the rim of the grasslands, one white, one the color of a fawn. The wind is shoving my bus around, but it is beginning to feel cozy in here. I insert my tape of birdsongs. Curlews keen, gulls guffaw, tiny shorebirds bleat and shriek.

14

In the Time of the Birds

The early winter storm that ushered me into Topeka last night has blown itself away. When I turned south toward Cheyenne Bottoms a few minutes ago, I felt a bright new wind from the north centering up at my back. It is good to be back on a two-lane road again. The world of the interstate always feels prepackaged, even the scenery. While the towns around here are only three or four buildings strong, they stand up proudly, one of a kind. In between them, central Kansas billows gently, sage green under an oyster sky.

After Hargrove, the cattails appear, islands first, then dark rivers of wands waving in the wind. I am looking for the sign the ranger mentioned on the phone. He said it was easy to miss. Just when I think I must have driven too far south, I spot a great blue heron standing solemnly by the road. Automatically, I step on the brakes. But it is not until I come to a full stop that I see the small wooden sign beside the bird. "Greetings, Mom," I say to the bird. "Thank you!"

I turn onto the gravel and clay dike, and a flutter of anxiety whirs in my chest as the bus slides sideways toward the edge.

A scant layer of snow has transformed the hard clay into slime. The ranger had cautioned me about this possibility, but I could not turn back now if I had to: four great blue herons have risen on my right. They hang in the air over the dike, still as an Audubon print, then lower into the reeds. Did they flap their wings at all?

A large wooden box stands at the first crossroads. From it I extract a map of the great looping maze of dikes. A commitment to right-hand turns seems to be the only way to keep from getting lost. I make the first of them gingerly, hovering on the cusp of a stall. The bus tracks perfectly; there is just enough gravel mixed with the clay to produce friction. I shake out my shoulders and try to relax.

As I move farther into the marsh, the cattails spiral about the bus like a dark galaxy. The birds are all around me too, garlanding the sky in pulsing strands, distant and fine. At times they flow out of the canals as I drive by, so close I can see their pinions fingering the air currents.

I pull over to watch two northern harriers, working low over the cattails, their white rumps flashing as their long, strong wings power them into wingovers and chandelles. One drops down on his prey in full stall, falling out of the sky as if shot through the heart. A fraction of a second before the grab, he flares, extends his talons, then nails his target like a remote-controlled missile hitting a silo.

When I reach the center of the marsh, I park by a group of mudflats. Three o'clock. Three more hours of light. Before me, weaving like a giant creature, thousands of avocets, dowitchers, greater yellowlegs, and sandpipers are bobbing, throbbing, crying, and leaping suddenly into the air for reasons I cannot determine.

My friend Jay, who runs the nature center in Canton, told me that shorebirds from as far west as the Aleutian Islands

and as far east as Greenland funnel down to this very marsh
so that they can rest and fatten up for the long haul to Central
and South America. I had expected to see a lot of birds, but
nothing has prepared me for this prehistoric pageant in central Kansas.

Beside the flats, just to the left of the bus, two white-faced
ibises stalk in unison on the soft mud, their long sickle-
shaped bills raised haughtily, their mahogany feathers bur-
nishing as the light angles their elegant bodies. I slide out of
the bus and creep toward them, hunching down behind some
reeds. When I get about fifteen feet away, they begin twisting
their necks and fluffing their feathers. I halt and slowly lower
myself onto my heels. Before long, they resume their posing
and probing. I recognize these birds, have seen their sacred
images on the walls of Egyptian tombs, have read that their
mummified bodies lie beside those of the pharaohs in the
stillness of their pyramids. I feel honored to be in their living
presence. Obviously the ibis has figured out what it needs to
know about immortality. I mean, here they are in Kansas of
all places. Right under my nose!

When they finally lift up into the sky, the eye of my mind
takes off with them. I see the delicate wrinkling of the Rock-
ies to the west, the filigree of riverbeds, the soft flesh of the
plains. "Beautiful," I announce involuntarily. My voice, no
more than a whisper, spreads out in all directions like a radio
signal; there are no edges to this marsh.

It must be getting toward five because the entire marsh is
now shot through with alpenglow. I have begun to make my
way toward the western entrance. I am disappointed that
camping is prohibited in the marsh, even though I understand the reasons for it.

When I round the last and outermost loop, I come upon a
small coyote standing in the middle of the dike. She watches

me approach calmly, confident that I will stop. I halt the bus about twenty feet from her, and we regard each other for several seconds. I am close enough to study her dainty features, the lovely stippling of her blond-and-russet tones.

Hoping to detain her, I stick my head out the window and begin speaking to her in the low, coaxing language of mothers. She listens to me, head cocked, ears high, her soft eyes level, fixed just beyond me. Then she turns away from me and very deliberately begins trotting down the middle of the gravel road, looking back every few seconds like a child checking on its parent. Taking my cue, I let out the clutch and fall in behind her. We travel like this for about a hundred feet when suddenly she freezes. I pull up just a few feet behind her. Her whole body seems to be riveted to a point a few feet to the left. Abruptly she pounces. It is an unbelievable leap, arcing from the center of the road to the brush without a sound, without even disturbing the grasses. I call out to her, quite beside myself with admiration. Her small face pokes up out of the high grass. No trophy. She trots back onto the road, collects me with a quick over-the-shoulder glance, and off we go again, the hunter and her large blue support vehicle.

We hunt together like this for nearly half an hour, she springing gaily at phantoms in the grass, while I, feeling oddly compelled, trail along after her like a devotee. When we reach a small copse to the left of the dike, she simply dissolves into its shadows. I halt there in the apricot light for a few minutes, savoring the fine magic of this encounter.

Heading down the final stretch of dike, I begin to deposit the afternoon into my tape recorder. "Can there be anything more to this day, anything more wonderful than the last few hours of my life?" I ask. At that very moment, I notice that I am traveling down the dike with hundreds of monarch butterflies. Although they are riding the fresh wind from the

north, my bus in first gear is moving slightly faster, and I have
to ride the clutch to keep from injuring them as they slide up
and over my windshield. Out to my left, I notice a swarming
of butterflies near a small green tree. I drive just beyond it,
park, and turn around to see what is going on.

The entire leeward side of the tree is teeming with autumn
colors, butterfly leaves, ablaze in the last rays of the sun. I
quickly forget about the approaching night. Through my
binoculars, I watch them try to gain purchase on the quaking
boughs. They hover like hummingbirds until the leaves calm
down a bit and then make a grab. Sometimes it takes several
tries to get a tight grip on a leaf. Once firmly attached, they
become part of the tree, bouncing and shaking in the wind.

I have read about butterfly trees, these ancient inns that
mark the migration routes of the monarchs. Knowledge of
their locations, like the route itself, is passed along with the
genes. In his book *The Endless Migration,* Roger Caras points
out that even though the ancestors of these monarchs issued
from the same high valley in the Michoacán mountains of
Mexico in early March, it takes many generations for them to
complete one yearly migration cycle. But the eggs left behind
on the milkweed pods along their route have within them all
the information the next generation will ever need—and the
next and the next—to find their way back to the valley.

The butterflies hanging on for dear life in Cheyenne Bottoms have never seen the Michoacán mountains, and they
probably never will. And yet, that one high valley in Mexico is
their alpha and omega, the reason for and the meaning of
their brief tenure on earth. Chances are they will never know
why they do what they do, or how their part fits into the
whole. Just like us.

When dusk finally settles into the cattails, obfuscating
everything that is not me and my bus, I start up the engine

and turn on the heater to warm up my hands and feet. But I am not ready to leave this place. In a strange way, it feels too much like my destination. *This is it,* I think, dropping my head into my folded arms on the steering wheel. *I'm there!* I sit, bowed over, for a long time, listening to the droning of the engine, trying to absorb the wonder of having crossed a vital threshold without knowing it—of having entered at last the heartland of my journey.

Driving down the main street of Great Bend a couple of hours after the Brass Buckles for Guys and Gals store has closed its doors for the evening is like trespassing in an Edward Hopper painting. The face of the two-story town is firm, like a parent who has just announced bedtime. The few people on the street seem leftover, unmoored, unaware that somewhere else, in lighted rooms, people are chatting comfortably, forks and spoons clinking.

Although my "campground" is no more than a place to park and pay, I really don't mind; I am too excited about tomorrow. I set my alarm for five-thirty, determined to be out on the dikes for the cracking of the dawn.

At 5:30 A.M. the world is black as tar outside the bus. Not a hint of light in the east. Clearly I have miscalculated the dawn by at least an hour. Great Bend, I then remember, is on the westernmost edge of the central time zone. It is bitterly cold. After starting up the engine, I have to yank the sleeves of my pile jacket over my hands so I can grip the steering wheel.

The inside of the doughnut shop is toasty. I can smell the fact that the heat is on for the first time. Sitting down at a table for four just inside one of two large black bay windows in the front of the shop, I imagine myself inside the Hopper painting once again, alone in an amber pool of light, writing on a legal pad, drinking coffee from a thick white mug. The four men bantering affably at the table by the other window seem only mildly curious about my intrusion into the hour that they own at the doughnut shop. For my part, I am happy to witness the center of their universe from the shadows.

By the time I head out into the marsh, the tip of the sun is directly ahead of me. Vermilion wildfire flicks along the horizon. The grasses beside the dike are tense and hoary. As the sun strikes them, the tiny crystals toss the light about, scattering the spectrum and blinding my eyes. The sound of my engine flushes pairs of ducks out of stationary rivers of mist. I am retracing my route of last evening, hoping to see the coyote again. When I pass the butterfly tree, I feel a tug of dismay. It is empty.

I am debating whether to stop and investigate when an enormous V of large white birds diverts my attention. They are white pelicans, fifty or more, their six-foot wings heaving in unison. Under them, backlit by the dawn, cormorants stretch out their batlike wings to the rising sun.

All of a sudden, I notice a dim form standing motionless on the dike a couple hundred yards ahead. Is it my sprite? Struggling along in first gear, heart accelerating, I lurch toward her, feeling like a teenager with a crush.

She blocks my path just as she did yesterday. I stop and we exchange brief glances. Then I look down and to the side, allowing her to study me. As before, she sets out in a slow trot down the middle of the road. I putt along behind her, stopping each time she intuits something in the grass. I am starting to worry because she keeps coming up empty. How can she survive? But she continues her aerial ballet without flagging, until at last, just a few feet off the road, she appears to nab something, for she is making small hippity pounces again and again in the same place. Finally she raises her head in triumph, the bloody back legs and tail of a gopherish animal draping from her mouth like a grizzled beard. Greatly relieved, I croon out my window like a mom as she settles into the task of dismembering the creature and then devouring it. She proudly displays each gory appendage before consuming it, and although her manners are revolting, I cheer every bite until she has quite finished.

She clearly wants us to continue hunting as before, but I, satisfied to know that she can take care of herself, am ready to get on to the mudflats and the swarms of waterfowl that must be waking up by now. Still, my eyes sting when I have to force her off the road and then witness her surprise in the rearview mirror, head cocked, questioning. As I work my way north through the cattail maze, I feel a soft longing reach out behind me.

The birds are just starting to unwrap when I pull up beside the flats: a wing, an oscillating head, the tucked-up leg poking out, then stretching way, way back. I leap out into the glistening morning, uncoil my own body, put my palms together, and bow to the sun. Then, because it feels so good, I bow again, this time to the birds. As I move around to the rear of the bus to get the Coleman stove and coffeepot, a maverick bolt of joy almost whacks me off my feet. *So this is what it's like to be alone!* It dawns on me that I can set up the stove right in the middle of the road if I want. So I do just that, to celebrate.

The coffee perks pleasantly while I get out my bird books, my binos, my windbreaker. Giddy with the sense of something ultimate, I stack these things up on top of the bus, fill my thermos with coffee, and then climb carefully up the front door onto the broad, flat roof. After settling into my Crazy Creek chair and pouring a steaming mug of coffee, I look around in all directions. I am the highest bump on the horizon. I am the center of the marsh and therefore the world. I am, at this moment, absolutely absolute.

When I finally climb back down the front door of the bus, my legs are very stiff. I must have been sitting motionless for a long time. I stick my head in the bus to check the hour. Four o'clock. "You gotta be kidding," I mumble, feeling totally disoriented. *Where have I been for the past eight hours?*

I take off on foot down the dike. It feels good to work my legs, and I swing my arms vigorously. The light is beginning to turn to gold again, the way it did yesterday. I am amazed that the passing hours did not register in my psyche the way they normally do. I know that I have been radically awake all day. I think of the splashing of the coots in the canal by the bus, the great wedges and twirls and sheets of birds arriving and departing the flats. It is all there in my mind in perfect focus, like the tip of a candle flame, every minute of it. I stretch my arms over my head and then touch my toes a few times. I cannot believe how wonderful I feel: as clear and still as the immaculate abyss above me.

I pack up the bus deliberately, enjoying the act of putting each item back in its place. This mindfulness reminds me how I feel after my annual New Year's Day retreat with my friend Sarah. On that day, we alternate sitting and walking meditation from dawn to nightfall. I am always acutely aware of the light brightening, shifting, and dimming, but after the first couple of rounds, my mind stops keeping track of the passing hours.

Today, when I slipped out of clock time, I entered into a much larger expanse of time, into a flowing forward of events unrelated to human needs. Like the waves of monarch butterflies, cycling through many generations to complete one annual migration, this time is a flying arrow, free of measure, free of us. Today the birds drew me into their time, sucked my entire consciousness through the lenses of my binoculars until I was perfectly empty on the one hand and absolutely present on the other.

I watch the brilliant sunset reverently, as if I might not see one again. If I had not already booked my flight to California from Colorado Springs, I would stay on in this place. I am aware of how deeply I have moved into the experience of being alone. When I set out so smugly on this trip, I did not understand that my ability to cope with solitude was determined by forgotten events, by ghosts both good and bad that could deploy at will whenever I ventured too near their haunts. But they appear to have dropped behind for now, allowing me to make peace with the space around me and its additional dimension of silence.

15

Intervals

Eastern Colorado is breathtaking this evening. Undercutting a sheet of stainless-steel clouds, the sun roams the prairie like a spotlight, highlighting gilded crests, darkened troughs. My campsite rests on the curl of a swell.

The twilight thickens softly. My favorite time. I feel the old thrill rising, the electrifying suspense of a hiding child whose seeker wanders near. At dusk the unexpected happens. Kids know this; they will do almost anything to remain outside on a summer night. To combat this, my father hung a ship's bell from the porch rafters of our summer house. Its sole purpose was to gather us in at night for bed. Each child in our family had a different code and a different bedtime. I was two slaps of the clapper. The deal I made with myself was that I had to go home if I heard my code. So every night, when the dusk reached a certain intensity, I would jump on my fat-tired bike and, pumping like someone possessed, fly away from our neighborhood, leaving a wake of hair ribbons, siblings, and dogs. I still feel this way most summer nights.

Now, sitting by my bus, watching the darkness seep in, I

find myself thinking about my upcoming visit with Rachel and remembering another sunset on a high prairie ten years ago. We two were on a spontaneous road trip to Wyoming during what we thought was a remission of her partner's illness. While visiting a mutual friend in Jackson Hole, she got the news that Crawford, the man she lived with and had loved for so many years, was going to die from the cancer he had been battling. Within hours of the phone call, we were packed up and on our way back to the East Coast.

Driving toward Cheyenne, we passed through the Shoshone reservation. Attempting to divert Rachel from her misery, I told her the story of Sacagawea, the courageous Shoshone woman who was the translator for the Lewis and Clark expedition when it crossed the Teton Mountains nearly two hundred years ago. I had read that she was buried somewhere on the reservation.

When we spotted a small cemetery set into a nearby hillside, it was Rachel who suggested we drive in and try to find her grave. Lurching up the rutted access road, I noted in my rearview mirror a large, low car following us. It stopped just below the cemetery, backed off the road, and then parked, facing us. Three people were sitting in the front seat and three were in the back. No one got out. Uncomfortable, but not sure why, we got out of our car and started moving up and down the rows of headstones, checking each one carefully. Six male forms slid from the other car and assembled themselves deliberately, leaning against it, arms crossed.

I called out to Rachel, "We have to get out of here now!"

She looked up at me, annoyed. "What's the matter?" She nodded toward the men. "I'm not going to let them bully us. We're not doing anything wrong." She went on scanning the headstones, her face set.

I walked briskly to the car and started it. When she opened

the passenger door, she did not get in right away. "They're probably just curious. What's the matter with you?" She was angry.

"Native Americans don't like anyone messing around with the spirits of their ancestors. Even other Native Americans," I responded.

"Oh," said Rachel, climbing into the car, "I didn't know." As we bumped back down the hill, I saw her shoulders sag again, and she disappeared back into her grief. The low car was ten feet behind us when we turned south on the main road, and like an angry watchdog, it stayed right on our bumper for the next few miles until we finally cleared the reservation.

A little later, just as the bloodred sun was sinking into the mountains, we found ourselves in the middle of one of the most spellbinding landscapes either of us had ever encountered. Monochromatic, rhythmic space, cut to the bone by the two-lane road, this place was empty the way the sky is when there are no clouds; it is an emptiness that has no absences. We stopped on a rise and rolled down the windows. The silence was stunning. Because there was no sign of life at all in any direction, we left the car sitting right where it was in the middle of the road and started climbing up the embankment. As we ascended, the fawn-colored hills pressed down the horizons, and the huge sun began to rise again. Noticing a faint dirt track threading into some higher hills, I said, "If we drove up there we could watch the whole sunset again."

Rachel faced me and nodded, her face wet and very sad. "We have four-wheel drive—let's just head uphill until we can't go anymore. I want to sleep on the ground tonight."

I nodded. It felt right. The landscape was as bald and direct as the reality we were trying to confront.

The track, probably left by a hunting party, was barely

passable, but we heaved and jolted higher and higher, pulled by the last blazing stripe of light crowning the tallest peak. A few hundred feet from the summit, the path steepened abruptly and then ended in a couple of deep ruts. Foraging in the trunk, we found two sleeping bags and an unopened bottle of red wine. No cups. No food. This was fine. We took off for the top in silence. The slope was steep, and the sandy soil gave way underfoot.

When we arrived, the sun balanced on the rim of the world for the last time that night. Then the shadow of the earth slid over us quickly, like a wing of a passing bird, covering everything but the horizon, which burned on, glowing hotter as the shadows deepened.

Rachel was sitting cross-legged, her elbows on her knees, her long patrician fingers, nails lacquered red and ringed with sapphires and diamonds, clasped around the gritty half-empty bottle of wine. She was crying steadily, crying and sipping.

"He sounded so tired on the phone. Wounded, like someone had just kicked him in the chest."

"Tell me exactly what he said," I replied, trying to help her take the news into her body. By now the embers were red and swollen, the night sky bruised.

Something scuttled in the sagebrush behind me and I whipped around. Darkness only. Then a sharp "breep" came from the right. More rustling, and then the nighthawks streamed out of the earth and filled the sky, black silhouettes folding and twisting and diving against the glow of the hot scar on the horizon. Like hands, I said to myself, Sacagawea's hands, signing a message to us, wing-fingers, night-words, etching a story into the sunset.

"She's trying to tell us something," I whispered.

"Who?"

"Sacagawea."

"What is she saying?"

"Something fluttering and very light, something beautiful. I don't think we're supposed to translate it."

When the last of the coals died out in the western sky and the nighthawks merged with the night, we burrowed down in our warm bags and slept.

Now, ten years later, I fall under the spell of the prairie twilight again. I have been sitting at my picnic table for a long time, savoring the half-light. I think about the way I have lived my life from adventure to adventure, stringing them together as closely as possible as if this would result in a perfectly crafted life. But it is the interval that draws my attention now, the uncommitted space between the day and the night, between the seasons of our lives, where we are neither here nor there, where there is only yearning and expectation, where transformations take place. I wonder why I have been so afraid of it.

The stars arrive one at a time, then in surges, multiplying until the sky becomes a skin of stars. I am reluctant to end the day. The luminous clarity I am experiencing will probably evaporate tomorrow when I board the plane for San Francisco. I feel sad, for I have grown accustomed to the time of the birds and the stars, to the silence that is spreading within me. I have never felt better. Although I am excited about spending time with Rachel after so long, I will not be alone again until next week. I wonder if I will be able to get back to this place again.

16

The Night Sea Journey

As always, Rachel is positioned right in front of the arrival gate, but back just a bit so she can see me before I see her. She looks wonderful in well-fitting white jeans and a white oxford cloth shirt, unbuttoned deeply at the neck. Over these, she's wearing a navy blue velvet blazer, probably a Salvation Army store find. Her still-short dark hair waves up and around as it pleases. She carries a purple helium balloon.

I feel a rush of pleasure upon seeing her again. Time with Rachel is exciting, like an unopened present. Our friendship weaves a complicated chemistry: attraction, wariness, empathy, fear. We trust each other on the final level but are guarded with each other. Like sisters, we know each other too well.

Waiting in the long curling line around the baggage carousel ignites a chain of memories reaching back into the fifties. Rachel and I waiting in line at Boston College to hear T. S. Eliot read his poetry; waiting our turns outside a Boston tattoo parlor to get tiny stars branded on our thighs—the first and last tattoos in our small New England college, declared the dean—waiting to get into the Met to hear *La Bohème*; wait-

ing in Bangkok for a flight to Kathmandu; and the last time
we were in San Francisco together, waiting at the police barri-
cades to get into the Democratic National Convention, our
delegate passes hanging around our necks, mine legitimate,
hers finagled. I remember getting a note from her on the floor
later that day. It said, "Pssst. Look over your right shoulder,
I'm in the American Samoa Delegation." She was.

The Pacific Ocean flares out below us as we bank onto
Route 1 south. Impossibly long lines of waves stripe seaward,
platinum blue in the setting sun. Rachel is speaking in long,
hurried sentences, as if she is delivering a prepared speech.

"Six weeks ago, I thought all the confusion of the past
nine years—since Crawford died—was over, that I had finally
settled down in California, and could get on with my writing
and my life. I had hung up all the pictures; I was starting to
ask people over for dinner; I was getting involved in Quaker
meeting; and I was running the soup kitchen at the shelter for
the homeless where I'm on the board. Now everything is coming apart . . . I don't know anything anymore."

As she drives and talks, she holds her head very still, her
eyes bolted to the road. But her beautiful hands roam around
like small animals, scuttling across the radio dials, leaping
from the steering wheel into her hair, fooling with a thick red
piece of yarn she keeps tied to the gearshift. I can feel a new
horror story unfolding. *Damn!* I mutter inside. *I don't want to
hear this.* Her hands tell me she knows what I am thinking, but
she goes on resolutely.

"I met Marcus at the shelter when I was out here visiting
my friend Carole last winter. He was very drunk, but he inter-
ested me immediately. Who, I wondered, is this beautiful
man? Why is he here? I learned he was a Vietnam vet, an alcoholic, and that he lived 'down by the river' with some other
vets. The writer in me was dying to hear his story, but I stayed

away from him because"—she pulls in a long breath—"as you know, I swore off trying to save people. After Peter—you remember, the kid I tried to help—ended up robbing me, I felt so tapped out I had to call it quits. Anyway, I knew this man Marcus was definitely someone to avoid. And when I came back in the spring, he was gone. 'Good thing,' I said to myself."

I study her as she talks. Rachel's attractiveness is hard to pin down. All her features are irregular: Her small brown eyes are trimmed like an Eskimo anorak with long bushy lashes. Below is an asymmetrical but straight nose and a wide mouth, the lower lip wider and bigger than the upper. These attributes, set in classic proportions on the oval disk of her face, invoke an odd and memorable beauty.

She continues her recitation almost as if I'm not there. "Then one day in August, just after I moved here for good, he reappeared, sober. He had just spent sixty days in jail, in solitary confinement, which he had requested, on a trumped-up charge of arson. Arson, according to Marcus, is the way the local cops deal with homelessness. He appeared at the shelter every day, polite, self-composed. We began to chat after the noon meal. I was, of course, fascinated to meet someone who would talk to me about living on the streets. We didn't talk about the war, not then. After a while, I found myself looking for him around town. There were a number of chance and not-so-chance meetings. One day, he took me 'down by the river' to show me where he lived with the other vets."

She goes on to describe the men she had met in a clearing in the woods not far from the center of town. She and Marcus had come upon them, sitting around a smoldering fire, talking quietly and sipping beer from large brown bottles. Several stood up as they entered the fire circle, addressing Marcus ceremoniously. Then all of them shook hands with Rachel. She tells me that one man, wearing an Aussie hat with the front rim tacked up and a shark's tooth around his neck, was called Click-Click because he was the one who put the bodies in the body bags. Turning to me for the first time, she adds, "When you snap their dog tags shut, they go 'click click.'"

She glances at me again, knowing that she has me percolating. She is right. I have dozens of questions I want to ask about the men in the woods, but I don't ask them because I know this is not what her story is really about. I nod for her to go on.

"About that time, he began to drink again. When I brought up the subject of detox, he told me terrible stories about the treatment centers he had been in. He said he would never submit himself to that kind of abuse again."

She pauses, gropes for the frayed strand of yarn. Her dark red nails pulse at it for a moment. Then, with a shrug, she says, "So I made a deal with him. I told him that he could come home with me to detox, and that I would help him get on his feet and off the streets . . . as long as he stayed sober." She turns to me for my reaction, this time looking directly at my eyes.

Something slumps inside me. We have been through this before, but holy God, she keeps upping the ante. This is a bloody disaster. I don't say this to her, though; she is much too fragile. Aware of the weariness in my voice, I reply, "I've seen this coming for a while from the small bits about Marcus in your letters. Mostly from your silences."

"I know it's never really worked out in the past, but somewhere, deep down, I still believe that if you give someone like Marcus what they need, if they can have the same resources we have, they can make it."

Squaring for a confrontation, I interrupt her. "I don't know if that's true or not, I only know what happens to you, to your life, Rachel, when you take responsibility for someone else's life. You get derailed. Every time." I see her body toughen up. I should stop at this point but I don't, even though she is repelling my words. "I know you're trying to be a good person, but you're trying too hard. All you ever get back for your efforts is disappointment, depression . . . shit. Not to mention the fact that you have to start your life all over again." She is clenching the steering wheel with both hands now, her elegant rings jutting out from her fingers. "I'm sorry," I say. "You know all this. Keep going."

Pumping her body back and forth, she begins talking again. "He moved in about two months ago. At first I went on with my life, writing my column for the paper, seeing friends. When my grandchildren came to visit, I rented him a room; he's staying there right now as a matter of fact, while you're here. Anyway, for a while things went along nicely. He was sober. He did a lot of fixing up around the house and yard, spent several hours every day sculpting beautifully detailed figures from semiprecious stones, and he went to A.A. meetings regularly.

"After a couple of weeks, we began to talk in earnest. At first it was just for an hour or two after breakfast. Then we started spending the evenings talking, and finally the afternoons. I turned off my answering machine. Stopped working at the shelter, seeing friends. We began talking all night. We were both exhausted but we couldn't stop once the war came into it. After ten days with almost no sleep, I knew I was way over my head, especially when I started to encounter his anger. He must have known it too because he started drinking again."

She swings the car hard to the right and we pull into a parking space before a small seafood restaurant. I have been so absorbed in her story that I failed to notice we had entered the wharf area of a small town by the ocean. Shutting down the engine, she announces in a bright voice, "They have great oysters here. Roasted on the half shell, a little vinegar, chopped onions. Wonderful."

She orders for us: oysters, Greek salad, and a basket of crusty bread. As the robust platters arrive, she raises her glass of wine, bows slightly, and says, "Be sure to dip the bread into the sauce after you eat the oysters. That's the best part." She waits until the waiter has finished serving us before resuming her story. "By then I was absolutely determined to make him well, but I knew I couldn't do it alone. So I pulled some strings and got him into a good detox center not too far away. I spent time with him there every day, went to group meetings for the families, the whole thing.

"It all fell apart when I went to Hawaii for a wedding. Because he was doing so well in detox, I decided to extend my trip for a couple of weeks. I was beginning to feel incarcerated myself, as if I were living in a cave. During my second week away, my friend Carole, who was watering my plants for me, found him in my house. Drunk. She told him to leave and called me right away. I felt like I had been kicked in the stomach. I guess I really had been because I got really sick that day, fever, stomach cramps, the shakes. I was desperately ill coming back on the plane. By the time I got home, I barely had the strength to go out looking for him. . . . He's sober again. Living in my house again. But I don't know how long I can do this. And I don't know how to stop it."

Bright morning sunshine sifts through the eucalyptus trees around Rachel's patio. Strange birds are crying. I have set up my laptop on a glass-topped table, and beside it, a cup of coffee, whitened by hazelnut Cremora. Not as bad as it sounds. Rachel is off taking Marcus to the dentist. I am grateful she has spared me the discomfort of his presence so far. Even so, last night was laced with dreams of thick jungles, dim forms stalking, odd pieces of uniforms, as if by taking over his space in the house, I had inherited his dreams. When morning finally came, I found myself wishing I was back in the blue bus, following the birds.

I have been watching the world so deliberately since I left home that I have developed a habit of magnifying everything I see. Now I wish I could stop it. From the moment we entered this house last night, I have been distracted by signs of Marcus everywhere around me. Little signs: the dent of a recent head in a lacy pillow on the guest room bed; a chain of small metal balls with the airborne wings attached, heaped on the dresser; cigarette butts, hastily dumped in the wastebasket; and now beside me on the patio table where I write, a beautiful little cross carved from soapstone, shards of jade and alabaster, and a fine chisel set down before the other chair exactly so, as if he has just gone into the house for a cup of coffee.

I know already that this part of my trip will not be about the birds, even though they are flowing down the coast a few miles away. Marcus's presence has eclipsed them, just as it has eclipsed what had been Rachel's life. Last night after finishing her saga, she asked me how trying to help someone could possibly be wrong. This morning I ask myself the same question. My feelings puzzle me. How is it that in just sixteen hours, this poor man I've never met has become the enemy?

Point Lobos, one of the great headlands of the world. Here waves rolling in from Japan collide with brute pinnacles of granite and shoot fifty feet into the sky. On a small outcropping seaward of the peninsula, sea lions lumber onto the rocks, throw their heads back, and howl into the thunder of the waves. I have been watching a pair of seals surfing the huge waves into a small cove, hurtling themselves like rag dolls onto the pebbled beach, then scooching back artfully into the waves to do it again. On the leeward side of a tall island about fifty feet away, brown pelicans and cormorants preen sedately. Western gulls, oystercatchers, and stilted sandpipers poke through the seaweed collars of sandstone rocks. Below me, sea otters gaze up doe-eyed from pulsating beds of kelp.

My senses are getting bombarded. I long to empty my consciousness and slip into the world of the birds as I did in Kansas, but Rachel is with me, and even though she has gone for a walk to give me some time alone, I cannot focus. The tension between us is too pronounced, and I am aware that this outing together is taking place during a short window in the day, between the time she took Marcus his breakfast and deposited him at the medical clinic and the time she has to return to town, pick him up, and drive him to an A.A. meeting early this evening.

At noon we find a level spot high on a cliff above the surf. Here we eat fresh mozzarella and tomato sandwiches and share a large bottle of cranberry juice. We try to talk of ordinary things, my trip, our children, but we are out of balance and we know why. He sits between us on the rock, a specter, obstructing our view of each other, stilting the conversation. He is there with us in the car too, as we drive back to town along the breathtaking coast.

But Rachel is still trying hard to make my visit special. She has just pulled a roast chicken from the oven and is placing it on the beautifully set table in the dining room. As I light the candles, I admire the lovely old silver, the heavy linens, and the bowl of exotic purple flowers at the center of the table. I am moved that she has made such an effort for me tonight. Just as we are sitting down to eat, the phone rings in the kitchen.

"He needs a ride home from his A.A. meeting," she calls from the kitchen doorway. "I'll be back in fifteen minutes."

I am on the phone talking to David when they come through the front door, she, head down and forward, walking toward the kitchen with a determined step, he, tailgating her like a bad child, almost tiptoeing.

"A friend of his has died," Rachel announces as I reluctantly join them at the table. Without introducing us, she continues in a quivering voice, "I said he could come and be with us for a while." He sits demurely, eyes down.

"I'm not going to eat," he mutters in a barely audible voice.

"I'm sorry your friend died, Marcus," I say, looking at him for the first time. He nods. I recognize him at once. I have met this man in shelters in Hartford, and sitting on the steps of churches in New York. This man is not the enemy, he is a wound.

Abruptly he turns to me. "And who are you, Anne, friend of Rach?" He stretches his head out into the space between us, punky blue eyes demanding mine. "Important Anne of old, old friendship." Once handsome, his face has been melted down by alcohol and the streets: skin ruddy and thick, eyes recessed into their sockets, upper teeth gone (this fact nearly concealed by a neat military-style mustache). His speech is syntactically confused, slurred. I cannot tell whether he is drunk or drugged or both.

His aggressive tone alarms Rachel. She squares her body with the table, pushes her chair back, and raises her glass. "Tonight two very important people in my life are sitting at my dinner table. This is a very happy occasion for me. I salute you both." She raises her glass to each of us.

But she cannot wrestle the evening back from him. After refusing to eat with us, he sits between us, his open jackknife in his left hand, jabbing the chicken as he continues speaking. "I can tell you this. She's never going to meet a man who can take care of her like I can. She's never going to have a better friend than me." Once again he puts his face right in mine. "You know why? Because I know women. Just like I know animals." He drags his right forefinger under his nose. "I can smell what they're thinking. I know where this woman is, even when she is on the other side of town. When she gets near, I have her right in the crosshairs of my rifle." He draws his arms up and aims across the candles at her. "Right where I want her."

Rachel reaches over and touches his shoulder gently. "Enough," she says firmly.

But he can't stop; he is too wired. Rachel droops in her chair. He is talking to her alone now. "All you have to do is keep focused. On me. On us. On what we have to teach each other. That's all. Nothing else." Rachel is staring blindly at something over my head.

Abruptly he swings his body around and faces me. "And what is your opinion about *this* friendship, Important Friend of Rach?"

I stare dumbly in front of me. I can't believe this is happening. It takes me a moment to realize that I am terrified. I look around the formal dining room, seeking reassurance from the dark oil paintings of Rachel's ancestors, the antique tables and sideboard that once presided in stately homes along the Atlantic coast. The contrast of past and present only makes the present more surreal. Crazier. His face is still thrust into mine.

"I don't have one," I say sharply, trying to back him off.

He doesn't accept this, prods harder. "You do, and I know it. I know these things. I know what people are thinking. You don't like it. I know that."

Accused. I hold my ground. "Relationships are based on

chemistry. I can't possibly know the chemistry of your friendship with Rachel." But I do and it scares me.

Later, after she has driven him back to where he is staying, Rachel admits that she cannot hold up much longer. "I'm thinking of trying to get him settled somewhere south of here, where it's warmer in the winter and there are better services for homeless people . . . as soon as we finish the application process for assistance, and he gets his new teeth."

She is clearly worn out. Even so, I have to say it out loud. "You're going to have to be very careful, Rachel." She plays with her rings, turning them round and round. I wait for her to look up. She refuses. I go on. "Especially when you begin to separate from him." When she finally does look up at me I add forcibly, "I mean it."

"This is so hard," she replies in a flat voice.

The morning sun shifts in and out of the trees, falling lightly on my back as I write at the patio table. Because the air is slightly chilly, a part of my mind stays focused on the exquisite warmth between my shoulder blades. Rachel is about to leave, with a wicker basket over her arm containing oranges, bananas, milk, and cereal for Marcus's breakfast. She seems perky, upbeat. Last night has been erased from her mind.

"I went over earlier, and he's feeling much better this morning. It was the shock of losing his friend. He isn't usually like that."

I can only nod. I look at what I have written in the past two days. Why have I spent so much time detailing this sad, frightening story? What does it have to do with migration, with this journey I am on?

An answer to this question surfaces with the image of the sea on a moonless night, dark on dark, reflecting nothing. I am reminded of the myth of the night sea journey. Ancient people living by the Mediterranean Sea believed that when the sun entered the sea each night, it had to do battle with monsters and demons seeking to devour it. Every morning, when it rose in the east triumphant, people celebrated its heroic rebirth. This pattern recurs again and again in early maturation stories: the youth descends into the underworld, combats the forces of evil, and if he is successful, is reborn a hero. If he is not, he drowns in the night sea. As I think about Rachel and Marcus, a third possibility presents itself: the hero becomes trapped in the night sea, fighting the same demons over and over and over.

When she comes back from breakfast, Rachel suggests that we drive up to Berkeley to hear Thich Nhat Hanh, the revered Buddhist monk, speak at the university. This would mean spending my last night up there in a motel. I am thrilled, not just to have a chance to hear this wonderful teacher, but to be leaving this house. As I pack up my things, I realize that my intrusion has not displaced Marcus at all; in fact, it appears to have strengthened his presence in the house, concentrated it. Watching Rachel move quickly about the house, shutting windows, grabbing clothes off the line, I understand that we are both fleeing.

Berkeley never really changes. I feel as if I have been standing in line with these people all my life; many of us now have gray in our hair. Strangers are talking to each other, reading from Thich Nhat Hanh's books. As always, a young woman with waist-length black hair offers me an orange. Although everyone knows there are only twenty-seven tickets left, no one displays anxiety or impatience about the long wait. We are bound by a general agreement: that it is a privilege to be standing here in the afternoon sun in Berkeley, California, with the promise of hearing the gentle monk from Vietnam before us.

*   *   *

After the teaching is over, Rachel and I walk in silence until we find an open restaurant. She seems very far away.

"You heard it, Anne," she says at last as we settle into a booth. "What could possibly be wrong with trying to help someone?"

I am tired. It is too complicated. "I don't know, but I know you're going to do what you're going to do, no matter what anyone says."

She snaps her head angrily. "You bet I am!" And then, almost spitting out the words, "You bet I am!"

We sit in silence, surprised by the vigor of this exchange. The situation clarifies slowly. I believe that Rachel is in danger. I don't care about the nobility of her actions or the sense of purpose her commitment has given her life. I just want her to stop what she is doing. The pinched expression on her face tells me she cannot stop—that if she did, her life would lose its meaning, its design.

After we have finished eating, she breaks the silence. "Thich Nhat Hanh says that if we practice compassion in all that we do, our lives and the lives of others will change for the better. That's what I've been trying to do, and everyone treats me like I'm crazy. I just don't get it. How *do* you help someone?"

I think about his message that evening, so simple and yet so terribly complicated. "What he said," I reply, "is that the greatest gift you can give another person is your presence."

We sit quietly for a while, pushing bread crumbs around on the polished wooden table. The whole situation seems ludicrous. This man needed so much more. But how was he going to get it?

17

On the Road Again

We entered the storm right after taking off from San Francisco and remained inside of it for what seemed like a long blood-sloshing time. But now we have broken out on top and the airplane is radiating with light. I look around; people are reading mostly. A few talk. Through my window I note the ghostly peonies blooming capaciously along the leading edge of the front. I wait until we are over a big one, then jump out the window. A cold blast of air knocks me head over heels. I arch my back to stabilize, then draw in my arms and go sizzling through the sky like a meteor. This is something I always do when I fly above the clouds. I can't help it.

For the past half hour, I have been trying to get into Tim O'Brien's much-acclaimed *In the Lake of the Woods*, which David gave me just before I left. But it is about a Vietnam vet losing his mind, a coincidence I can't cope with at the moment. Besides, Rachel's insistent eyes keep flicking on and off in my consciousness like the light from a failing projector on a screen. She will not let me turn away from Marcus, keeps shaking his presence in front of me like a rattle.

She knows I know what her relationship with Marcus is all about. The fascination, the fear. These are the margins of a life, my life at least. She also knows I know how dangerous it is when these two begin to merge like a moth and a flame. Or splice together, as they did in the form of my first husband. Who am I to tell her how to live?

He was my flight instructor. Silver-haired, silver-tongued. The one who flew me out over the Atlantic Ocean so I could watch the stars wrap around the plane, the one who taught me how to loop the loop. Boy did he ever.

And then, after we were married, the one who kept me up on a knife's edge for eight years. He did this with illusions and cunning. Poetry and mockery. Bluff and guile. I was paralyzed by possibilities, by a terrible need to believe his stories because the truth was much too threatening.

There were five real children caught in our house of mirrors. Our two girls. His three boys. He must have been amazed at what I would buy into. I am, looking back. A woman who has five pairs of innocent eyes latched on to her for dear life will do the fandango on the head of a pin if she has to. As long as she believes that she is doing it for their sake.

I don't think he could stop himself, really. I must have been addictive, like potato chips. Instead of quitting while he was ahead, he had to keep inventing new and more dramatic ways to keep me on my toes. When I stopped believing his new stories, he began taking the old ones back: "Remember that story I told you about spending Christmas on a Pacific island during the war?"

"Yeah," I responded, shaking my head sadly as I pictured him standing guard in a tropical downpour, eating his ration of plum pudding out of a can while listening to the faint sound of soldiers' voices singing "Silent Night." I had been

very moved by this vignette of the war. I looked up at him.
"You even cried when you told me."

He looked directly at me, his steel gray eyes aimed straight
at my soul, and then he said in a casual semidrawl, "Well, it
wasn't true."

Like that.

I learned the subtle art of dormancy. It was easy once I got
the hang of it; I could numb out in a flash and still cook dinner for seven. He was the only one who knew. He'd say, "Your
eyes are dead. You're not listening to me."

"I'm listening," I'd reply. "Go on." But I was not. How
can someone force you to hear? At night I would lie in my
bed, still as a sarcophagus, until his breathing leveled out.
Then I would let my mind go to its camp on the Nepal side
of Mount Everest, just below the Khumbu icefall. I would
imagine myself waking sometime after midnight, dressing
very quietly so I wouldn't wake the other climbers. Outside
the tent, the cold was deep and clean, the inky sky dazed
with stars. As I set off up the winding route through the icefall, I could hear the rhythmic crunch of my crampons on
the hard snow, the light clinking of the carabiners clipped
on to my harness. Up and up and up I would go, the stars
pulsing softly all around me, the cold vibrating like a cathedral organ, the huge mountain, luminous and holy, burning
blue as if lit from within. I would keep moving upward,
aimed at the stars, until I fell asleep. Night after night I did
this.

Eventually he wore me out. Which of course he was bound
to do. It happened shortly after I threatened to leave if he
did not agree to marriage counseling. He consented—with
unmasked contempt. During one of the few sessions we
attended together, the doctor suggested that he take up a
physical activity to help work off some of his anger. "Why not

chop wood?" he had asked. "That's what I like to do when I feel frustrated."

Two days later I found a brand-new ax leaning against the wall in our bedroom. I did not say a word about it. I just picked it up and took it out to the toolshed in the backyard. The next day it was back in the bedroom, in the same spot. It was just another game. I knew that. But I was too weary for a new set of rules.

No wonder it was so painful for me to watch Rachel zeroing in on her flame, knowing as I do that the story is really about the moth. The flame is simply there, filling a void. It's astonishing, really, the people who will show up when there is a void around.

I lost her at the San Francisco airport after going in to check on my flight. There was very tight security, and the attendants kept pushing me forward. No matter what I did, I couldn't get back to her to say good-bye. It was a fitting conclusion to my four days with her, not being able to reach her one more time.

As the airport shuttle bus jostles toward the south overflow parking lot in Colorado Springs, I scan the rows of cars. Finally I spot the blue bus, standing high and alone like a queen, veiled by a thin layer of red Colorado clay.

I climb through the sliding door, jubilant. "I'm home!" I announce to my stuff. Everything is as I left it. The bird books lined up neatly on the backseat next to my Books on Tape. The small state-of-the-art thermos David bought me for the trip. The watercolor Anee sent me just before I left is still posted on the wide dashboard. It shows the Dalai Mama, as she likes to call me, driving the blue bus across a western desert, singing "On the Road Again" at the top of her lungs.

In the lower left-hand corner, a little coyote peeks out at the viewer, as if to say, "Will you look at that!" How did she know about the coyote?

I open the windows and the sliding door and unfold myself onto the couch, flipping my feet up on the coffee table box. How in just four days had I gotten so far away from all this, from the gorgeous silence of my trip?

Interstate 23 southbound is free of traffic by the time I head south. At this clip I could make it to Taos and Anee tonight. But I really need the silence now, the crisp cold night; I need to wake up in the blue bus alone.

I flow back into my journey slowly, mile by mile; the last four days fade from my consciousness, like a rugged detour, like a rugged marriage.

I slide a tape of Mozart's horn concerti into the tape deck. The music is clean and huge, like this Colorado night, enameled with stars and planets, silver, blue, gold, coppery red. There are no towns, no cars, no lights here. Not one thing at all to disturb the uncorrupted splendor of the night. I let go of my mind entirely. It bolts away like a dog off the leash.

18

Sea Change

Full fathom five thy father lies;
  Of his bones are coral made;
Those are pearls that were his eyes;
  Nothing of him that doth fade
But doth suffer a sea-change
Into something rich and strange.

WILLIAM SHAKESPEARE, *THE TEMPEST*

Ninety miles to Taos and then five more to Anee's village. This will be the first time I have seen her since she moved to New Mexico four months ago to begin a new life as a painter at the age of twenty-nine. Even though I now fully support what she is trying to do, I am apprehensive. The life she left behind in Wyoming was unquestionably limited as far as her career was concerned. Still, I had grown accustomed to the high peaks and log cabins, the early morning climbs up to high snow bowls for one perfect ski run before breakfast at Nora's, her seasonal jobs that barely paid for the privilege of being there. I had also become used to the angst I felt as I watched her struggle with the warring parts of her personality—cowgirl, artist, daughter, woman.

We'd fought when she was home in April. This was hard on both of us because Anee and I rarely fight. But she had seemed so exhausted, down on herself. For years she had been trying to keep painting at the center of her life by working part-time, construction or landscaping by day, waitressing by night. Although she had learned to get by on very little money, she was tired of being so poor, and discouraged because she never had enough time to paint.

I guess I was frustrated too. I didn't know how to help her, and her relationship with her father was nonexistent. The term *starving artist* may sound romantic to some, but not to the mother of one. So when she abruptly announced that she was planning to become a full-time painter and open a gallery to market her work, I panicked. I couldn't imagine how she was going to manage financially, and given her low spirits, I couldn't envision where she would find the energy to pull off such an ambitious dream.

Graduate school, I kept thinking. *Teaching certificate. Graphic design. Benefits!* And then, with my solutions all lined up, I'd delivered the "get a real job" speech that had been on the top of my pile for several years. We had been on our way to meet our good friend Sarah for lunch when I launched into it, poor timing for sure. I remember driving round and round the little restaurant in Collinsville with Anee crying and chopping the air with her left hand. "Mom, you can't do this to me! You're drowning me!"

"No I'm not. I'm trying to give you information that you need to survive in the world. That's my job."

"You don't understand," she pleaded, putting her hands

over her face. "It's too heavy. I need you to believe in me, to tell me I can do it."

"Anee, I'm not saying you can't do it. You're the one who says you're sick of dumb jobs. The endless stream of roommates, never having time or a decent place to paint. What do you expect me to say to you?" I had finally parked the car behind the restaurant, where Sarah wouldn't see us and become concerned.

Anee then took a deep breath, collected herself, and said in an even voice, "Mom, the things you're telling me about are things I need to know. I respect that. But right now, they can't help me because they're *your* answers to *your* anxiety about *my* life. I know you would feel much better if I had a job that offered benefits. But I can't do it for you. Right now I need to find out if I can make it as an artist. That's all. Nothing else matters to me right now."

By the time we finally entered the restaurant forty-five minutes late, I was totally depleted. I had felt myself crushing her spirit, but this hadn't stopped me; I had been determined to say those things to her. As I sat there, jealously watching Sarah unpack Anee's dreams so carefully, so respectfully, I summoned the distance to wonder whether my speech had been for Anee's sake or for mine. She knew all that stuff. Maybe it was to clear my own conscience, my own slate of shoulds. Maybe out of guilt and insecurity, I was trying to parent her as a father might. After all, I had never asked myself to take a job because of the benefits. After all, I was the one who had posted Goethe's famous couplet on the bathroom mirror for them to grow up by:

Whatever you can do, or dream you can, begin it.
Boldness has genius, power, and magic in it.

When I looked across the table at the strain on my daughter's face that day, my spent diatribe seemed empty and self-serving. What she really needed from me was the force of my belief in her talent, and even more than that, the force of my belief in her ability to fend for herself in the world. It was all there inside of me. I determined then to show it to her.

Anee lives in that small New Mexico village we all have tucked away in our minds. I recognize this immediately as I follow the sweep of the S-turn that holds all the adobe walls and wooden porches together in a single forty-five-second image. Although it is late September, the windowsills and dooryards are still bursting with red geraniums, blue salvia, and red and yellow daisies. Hollyhocks reach all the way up to the roof beams. Many of the doors and windows are trimmed in an intense violet-blue that looks lovely against the warm tones of the dried clay.

Her house, soon to be gallery, sits behind and to the left of the bakery café at the hub of the village. It is a charming, funky two-story adobe structure with upper and lower porches. A hand-hewn ladder leans against the upper story, giving access to the flat roof. A stockade fence encloses a small garden, and sunflowers nod over the top of it as they doze in the sun.

On the door, a note:

IF YOU GET HERE BEFORE I DO
THE KEY IS IN THE CAT BOX
BACK BY FOUR

Passing through the small hand-carved door, I feel as if I am entering a jewel. Anee's paintings radiate all around me like stained-glass windows. I stand in the cool silence of the room. "It's okay, everything's okay," I hear myself saying over and over.

The newly whitewashed walls provide a crisp background for her work. She has set out glass jars of wildflowers on all the windowsills. In the far corner, a kiva fireplace with bancos to sit on creates a focal point for the room. Over it, she has hung a huge painting. A road opens the canvas. Beside it, the white mass of a house burns blue, the only anchor in shifting fields of turquoise, greens, and violet. I rotate slowly, round and round, the center point of a glorious kaleidoscope. Anee's gallery is utterly enchanting.

My relief is sudden and thorough. Feeling strangely exhausted, I stretch out in the sunspot on her bed like Goldilocks and let my mind disintegrate. There on my daughter's bed, I sleep out the creases left by my trip to California and my anxieties about her life.

This morning Anee woke me before dawn. "Ama, here is your coffee," she said, bending over my mattress in front of the fireplace. "You have fifteen minutes before you have to take your bath. I'll start running it for you." When Anee is feeling tender about me, she calls me Ama (pronounced Ahmaa), the Nepali word for mother. I let her take charge as I lay deep in my sleeping bag, watching the remains of the fire throw rosy patterns on the ceiling. The coffee was hot and strong. Minutes later, as I slipped from the cocoon of my sleeping bag to the warmth of the tub, she said, "Now you have fifteen minutes before we have to go." Then she freshened my coffee. Daughters, I thought. How can you tell anyone about this huge love, this mythic kinship? Either they know it or they don't.

I thought about the poem Mandy, my twenty-six-year-old,

had given me on my birthday. It is about a moment she experienced at a dinner party we both attended some months ago. In the first stanza, she describes sitting across the table from me, watching me tell a story. She notes the candlelight flicking on my face, the lace tablecloth separating us. In the second, she maneuvers closer, saying, "Her hair always brown / I know its texture in my sleep. / The faint scent of her shampoo." In the third verse, she zooms in even closer with: ". . . her eyes, so light / The blue nearly lost/ Like mine." Finally she moves inside.

> And then, my heart nearly breaking,
> I am struck from the blind side
> By the awe,
> The honor
> To have come from within
> That which I hold highest.
> Most sacred.

Thinking about this poem in the predawn light, I had a strange out-of-body experience. Suddenly I became my daughter, watching a stranger in the candlelight. The stranger was me, but it was also my mother: brown hair, blue eyes, an ankle turned under calf. Mandy's poem was telling me that my genes and their codes have moved along in time. My eyes, the tilt of my head, my poems, have already migrated. Astounding!

Anee was quiet as we drove up the dirt road to the zendo. It was almost dawn, and I could study her profile in the soft blue light. Her great mane of brown-and-gold hair was twisted into a knot at the back of her neck. With long long lashes, fine features, and a strong jaw, she seemed both delicate and fiery.

The shrine was small and lovely, set in a shallow bowl on

the side of a mountain. Around it were attractive gardens, and quiet places to sit or walk. Anee whispered to me as we removed our shoes outside, "The only thing really different is that here you face the wall."

As I entered the meditation hall, I noted that several people were already seated on the two platforms that ran along either side of the room. They were indeed sitting with their backs toward the center of the room, their heads only about fifteen inches from the smooth gray wall. It seemed pretty strange to me, but I copied Anee's motions carefully, bowing low to the Buddha, arranging my cushions, and bowing to the cushions, or maybe it was to the wall. When she turned and nodded, I stepped up onto the platform, sat down, crossed my legs, and confronted the wall.

And then the wall confronted me, nearly knocked me over backward. I was used to sitting before the window in my meditation room at home, in a world where tree branches shake on the surface of the pond and dry leaves flip and skid across the wooden deck. In the great monasteries of Nepal, one has to incorporate wildly ornate red and gold and blue temple painting, colossal golden Buddhas, incense and flowers, monks chanting, birds flying in and out, all this into the silence, the emptiness of mind. So I was used to the acts of incorporation, acts of separation.

But this wall was different. It sat a few inches from my face like a barricade, forcing my unquiet mind back on me. My thoughts didn't have any place to go, except back into my mind where they were not wanted.

I liked it there though, liked being with my daughter in the cool blue dawn. I could see her in my peripheral vision, a small compact Buddha, her body taut with characteristic intensity. I felt a smile rising in me as an image from her childhood popped loose. She was standing beside a palmetto palm in our backyard in Florida, her serious face screwed up in concentration, her muscular little body streaked with dirt and sweat. Above her droopy shorts, two grubby handprints on her shiny belly. Before her, Burgie, our black Great Dane, and Gino, our neighbor's garbage-eating boxer, were wrestling furiously in the soft dirt, reducing to shreds the bows from the Easter lilies and the little cotton nighties that she has spent all morning putting on them.

After that the wall backed off and lightness drifted through the zendo like petal showers from a blossoming tree.

Anee and I sit across from each other at a small restaurant in Taos. It is late. We have been up on her roof watching the sun drop into the mountains. In New Mexico this is like watching a volcano in reverse. We have been talking about her paintings, which are already selling well, even though the gallery is not yet officially open. We have been talking about where to hang the signs, where to place the pots of geraniums, what to serve at the opening.

When dessert and coffee arrive, Anee leans toward me, her face glowing in the candlelight. "I've been wanting to tell you about a dream I had a little while ago. It's about healing. And transformation, I think."

I nod to hear more.

"I was bodysurfing in the ocean in Rhode Island. Each time I rode a wave, I would end up in deeper water. It was okay. I liked the cool green interior of the sea, the fact that the waves were taking me there. Then I noticed Grandma gliding toward me, her dark blue eyes serious, but smiling. She paused before me and a dress of many colors billowed around her. We reached out and hugged each other, and then we kissed. I felt a surge of questions flow out of me, questions about her dying, about opening the gallery, about the way I struggle. At the same time I felt a powerful wave of understanding entering me. The questions were suddenly gone, finished, and with them, the tension, the sadness, and all the fear. All that was left was me."

Anee left before first light this morning, off to a wedding in Colorado. After kissing me lightly on the forehead, she had stoked up last night's fire, adding a couple of logs. As the lights trembled and flared on the ceiling, her dream stirred in me, entering my mind with astonishing clarity. As if sometime during the night it had become my dream, as if it had somehow brought about a "sea change" in me as well. I had been so troubled by the way I had put myself in the middle of her path when she was trying to find her way. My reasons for doing it were as foreign to me as the "get a real job" lecture I had forced on her. But her dream suggests a very different interpretation of my actions. Perhaps, as her parent, it was my role to challenge her, to play the part of the dragon in her journey through the night/sea. Perhaps it was her task to overcome my challenge. Most wonderful of all was the role of the grandmother, a part I may play one day, if I am lucky. Imagine!

When the sun finally worked its way into the room, I watched the forward edge of light creep across a painting of the Valdez valley, igniting the abstract blocks of color one by one: purple, deep blue, pink, peach, until a landscape organized itself for my eyes. I know that this is how Anee sees the world, in blocks of color. That she leaves it up to us to pull the images together. I marvel. How does she know how to do this?

*   *   *

The café is fuller than usual this morning. The storm that has lowered the sky for the past two days has moved on, leaving the air sharp and cool. The snow-covered ridges of the Sangre de Cristos rise up through the trees, reclaiming the village once again. The mood is festive: people lean against their cars sipping coffee and chatting; others gather in large groups around small green tables; children dart in the sunlight, feeding the sparrows. I sit on the periphery, sipping dark coffee, feeling the sun touch inside of me, and watching the village, Anee's village now, come and go. I am ready to head north to Colorado, to begin my vigil for the sandhill cranes. The cold front that just passed through Taos may indeed be towing them along, right down the backbone of the Rocky Mountains.

19

Scripts

The white-capped peaks of southern Colorado muse quietly in the blue afternoon, like a row of Buddhas. This is the day I always conjure when I dream about driving around the West. Except for the part about my bus, which has been behaving poorly for the past couple of days, as if it has grown weary. Or doesn't want to go home, something I plan to do after the sandhill cranes come through. The mechanic in Taos said it was probably the altitude. I hope so, because right now, on perfectly flat terrain, I have the pedal to the metal and I am going only thirty-five. The last bulge—an exaggeration but I don't know a flatter word—forced me to shift down into second gear. Huff and puff.

Alamosa morning sun. Last night I slept as if I were free-falling through the universe in my blue bus. I had lingered outside as long as I could, until the sky was evenly coated with starlight, until the sharp cold had worked its way through my down jacket, my wool sweater, and my cotton turtleneck.

Then I slipped into the bus, undressed in the dark, and pulled my chilly bag up around me. As I lay wide-eyed in the silver light, watching the stars glide behind the mountains to the west, I felt the great spin once again, felt myself, the bus, the planet, getting wrapped up by the stars. Felt the whole cocoon fall away into the night.

I feel marvelous this morning, even though the bus is clearly struggling. Heading into the Monte Vista Refuge, I make myself a promise: just one crane, then I'll get it fixed.

The fluting ridges of the Sangre de Cristo Mountains float like white grosgrain ribbons against an indigo sky. Within their circumference, high prairie and marshlands, duck-filled ponds nesting in the tall grasses.

A western red-tailed hawk has just risen up beside me to the left. He has a small snake dangling from his beak, arching and twisting stiffly like a piece of wire. I pull over to the side just as he settles on a fence post about fifteen feet ahead of me. Having nailed the snake securely to the post, he now tries to stare me down. We face off, eyeball to eyeball. I dare not blink. This is a test. If I move, so will he, away into the marsh. Our relationship feels treeless, ingenuous; he has all the cards.

Finally he feasts. Long slithery things trail from his bright red beak. He is having a fine time. So am I.

My mother seems close by today. This is not always so. I think of one day last summer when I found myself walking from one room to another in our summer house, her house, searching for something I could not name. All of a sudden I was overcome by a powerful desire to do needlepoint, something she did most evenings while we chatted or watched the evening news. I simply had to have a canvas and some yarn in my hands. Somehow I talked David into driving over to Mystic in the Friday afternoon beach traffic, waiting for me in a hot parking lot while I pored like a sleepwalker through racks of garish designs until I found what I was apparently looking for, a row of songbirds sitting on a branch.

That evening, sitting on the window seat where she used to sit, I began stitching a rose-breasted grosbeak, my right hand pulling the bright yarn through the canvas in long familiar arcs. Within minutes, the sense of urgency dissolved. I felt the steady thump of the Atlantic Ocean regulating my pulse, the thrust and tug of my needle.

Now, stationed before the gory hawk, I imagine her sitting next to me, ironed blue jeans, clean white sneakers, a small square of bright silk knotted at her neck. She would have loved this moment. She rather liked a bit of blood and gristle, as long as it fit in the scheme of things. As long as it wasn't ours.

When she was alive, she was the one who kept track of the weather and the tides for the family. I loved those mornings when she would peer at Nicki and me over the rim of her coffee cup, her eyes innocent but frisky. "Shall we go see who's hanging around in the marsh?" she would suggest innocently. Those were the days we saw wonderful birds: willets and black-bellied plovers, greater yellowlegs and little green herons. I never understood how she knew they would be there.

I can feel her guiding me now, bidding me to stop, to look carefully, to hold absolutely still.

The hawk offers me his imperial profile one more time, then flares up, angling off over the marsh. I follow him, winding around ponds, working toward some imagined center. I stop now and then, seeing lots of ducks but nothing bigger. Not a shadow of a crane.

Finally, I park on a grassy hilltop and get out. A gust of air lifts my hair and streams it out behind me. I can see the entire marsh from here, pale as wheat in the noon sun. Descending a bit to get out of the wind, I set down my pack in a shallow bowl overlooking two duck-filled ponds. The sun is strong. I peel off my pile jacket, my sweater. I push up my sleeves. Then I lie back against my pack and slowly eat my cheese-and-tomato sandwich. The bright wind swoops down out of the hills and puckers the surface of the water; dark messages speed toward me like echoes along a canyon wall.

Suddenly I miss my father. And those summers when I raced with him on his eighteen-foot sailboat. My father had dark wavy hair then, a wildly mobile forehead, and bright eyes that flashed like blue jays. I was just a skinny wire of a girl when I started to crew for him, a six-year-old cartwheeler on the beach when I wasn't a sailor. But I loved it when the wind blew up, really blew, and my father and I would go pounding toward the windward mark. "Hike out, Pansy!" he would shout as dark puffs came barreling down on us. "We gotta keep her flat." And I would arc every one of my fifty pounds out to windward, as if my life depended on it, the top of my head stretching for the water, taking every fourth wave smack in the face. This was a blue with cold, rope-burned hands, stomach muscles screaming kind of ecstasy. There is nothing like it. "Attagirl," my father would say, his face crinkling up around his eyes. "Attagirl. We got the mark. Made-in-the-shade."

Then we would whip around it, sails flapping, boom swinging, lines all over the place. "Let's get that pole up, Sweetie-pie," he would say as he let out the mainsail and opened his "downwind beer." Scampering up on the deck, I could hear his throat pop as he chugged down the first half of the beer, "the best part," he would always say with a sigh. As fast as I could without blowing it, I would carefully thread the metal point at one end of the wiskerpole through the grommet at the corner of the jib where the leads are attached. *Go slow,* I would whisper to myself. *Daddy says you have to go slow to go fast in a sailboat.* Then I would push the sail out to catch the wind, careful not to spill an ounce of it. Holding the jib lead in my teeth, I would carefully slip the hook at the other end of the pole into an eye ring on the mast. When I trimmed the sail just right so it bellied out nicely, but not too much, the boat would surge forward and my father would say, "Nice going, Pansy-pie. Now let's go get Ellis. Play your jib. That's it. That's it. Perfect! We're gonna take him."

The acute clarity of this memory, its sounds and smells and emotions, make my heart race as I lie in my shallow niche in Monte Vista Refuge. To have that whole experience inside, intact—even the way the navy blue bathing suit chafed me under the straps—seems unbelievable. My mind can only store so much. God knows what else is in there. What about the things I don't know I know? I think about the migration behavior of the New Zealand bronzed cuckoo, something I read about recently. The adults depart before the fledglings do, just leave. Then a month later, the young birds take off and fly west over the ocean for a thousand miles until they get to Australia. Here they turn northward and travel for another nine hundred miles, to a spot where they well may find their parents, fat and happy, all settled in. *That bird's brain can't be any bigger than my knuckle. Where do these scripts come from?*

"Any cranes?" a voice calls out from behind me. I whirl around. "Sorry," the woman in the tan windbreaker says. "I didn't mean to startle you. I thought you saw me coming up the hill."

"That's okay," I say, brushing myself off self-consciously.

"No. Not yet. But the ranger over at Alamosa said any day now."

She aims off over the hill with a wave. *After the cranes, I head for home,* I promise myself. It is a nice thought. A not-yet kind of thought.

20

The Cranes

CRANE . . . "observe the time of their coming" = obedience to the law of the Nature-god Yahweh . . . healing: in medieval English carvings we see cranes sucking the breath of sick men . . . related to the alphabet: Hyginus says that Palamedes invented many letters of the alphabet watching the wedge-shaped formation of cranes' flight.

AD DE VRIES,
DICTIONARY OF SYMBOLS AND IMAGERY

Another flawless Colorado morning. I'm sitting inside the bus, drinking freshly perked coffee, my laptop on my knees. It is very bright and very cold. Sometime in the night, I remember easing up into consciousness and a breathless stillness. Orion was passing over, his nebulae quivering in his sword. I sensed a movement at the window next to my head, but when

I raised my body and looked out, there was nothing there, only the spinning stars, bottomless space. Again, a little jerk, a slide, a crawl. I touched the glass near my face; it was deeply cold, like metal. "Jack Frost," I whispered reverently.

So go my nights in the blue bus in Colorado. A gray-haired woman has just passed en route to the bathroom in a red velour bathrobe, a flowered dop kit in her hand. I love how relaxed she is, walking around in her nightclothes. In a nearby RV, I see another older woman through her bay window. She is folding bedding. Her partner sits at the table in the sun, writing on yellow foolscap. The thick tube of folded pages at the head of the pad tells me that he probably does this every day while she tidies up. On the table in their window is a heavy stone pot of impatiens.

At the closed visitors' center in the Alamosa refuge, I meet four birders emerging from their car, binoculars around their necks, earth-colored windbreakers, sensible shoes. They tell me that last night at their campground they had heard the unearthly warble of the sandhill cranes. "They have tracheas that are five feet long," one of them tells me. "Like French horns!"

I feel exhilarated as I pack up for the day. They must be close. A dirt path takes me out into the marsh. Northern harriers swing low over the rushes like crop dusters, ending each pass with dashing wingovers. Two great blue herons lift, flap three times, then hold it, hold it, hold it until I am out of breath.

I walk energetically in the still, cold morning, enjoying the pleasant thrust and glide of my muscles, the gentle thud of my backpack against my spine, my larger-than-life presence in the world. At the center of it.

*   *   *

The cranes spiral out of the marsh as I dreamed they would. Like strands of DNA twisting up toward the first filaments of cloud. I drop to the ground, steady my elbows against my knees, and focus my binoculars. Then, sucking in a great breath, I soar out through the door of my mind into the time of the Bible.

Unbroken rivers of grass glide silently around sage green hillocks and sandstone bluffs. Fragile mists trace the paths of hidden estuaries, palpate the obsidian faces of deep ponds. In the vast emptiness of this ancient morning, dark silhouettes lift off, one by one by one, their exultation cracking the air like cathedral bells.

I hear my voice trying to contain the moment. "Perfect," I say. "Oriental." "Oh God," I say.

But the cranes are beyond the reach of words, a still point in the flow of fifty million years, where resolutions of weight and balance, of loft and breadth and tug, of black and gray and white, reach perfection in one unbelievable slash of bloodred on the crown of their heads.

Footsteps behind me. Suddenly I feel self-conscious, as if I've been caught flapping my arms or yelling. Which is likely. The man smiles broadly.

"The cranes," I say rather stupidly.

"I know," he answers. "I can't believe what I am seeing." Just then, four more rise. They flow like arrows in a low arc over the grasses, their long legs trailing. The stranger and I watch them together. Then we forget about each other for a long time because cranes are rising from all points of the compass.

Walking back to my bus, I learn something astounding from an encounter with two birders on the path. Hoping for a chance to talk about the cranes, I had asked them, as is customary, if they had seen anything interesting. "Well," said the white-haired woman in the green windbreaker, her eyes beaming mischievously, "we just saw a pair of white butterflies mating in the middle of the path back there." "How nice," I replied, surprised by her response. She went on helpfully, "They'll probably still be there when you go by . . . because, you know, some butterflies mate for an hour or more."

"Really?" I stammered.

"Really!" she replied, wiggling her eyebrows artfully.

I watch them round the bend, then head down the path toward the butterflies. The blessed couple are right where she said they would be, locked tight, tipping and ruffling like a white peony, the wind threading through their wings.

The first time I try to turn over the engine, it refuses. This is new. When it does fire up, a strange clittering noise begins to nag at me as I backtrack toward a dirt road I had noted earlier. I am heading for the high ground now, following a distinct urge to get into the bead of lapis lazuli where the cranes are flying. While I goad the faltering bus up onto the bluff before me, I am aware that I am pushing it too hard, but I just don't care. If I break down, I break down. All that matters is that I am exactly here in this place on this day.

Once I get the bus perched on the highest knob, I put my windbreaker and binos up on the roof. Then I climb up the left front door. It's tricky: right hand on gutter rail, left hand on top of the open door, right foot on the dashboard, push hard, dangle, scooch back, back, back until the roof is level.

The dimensions of my new vista are exhilarating. I stand up tall and stretch my body high and wide. I am surfing the crest of a huge wave. The marshlands roll out before me in long stripes, heading toward the blue mountains of a distant shore.

The cranes rise from below. Drops of blood, smoky wings, ebony tips. Their eerie warble swells as they pass by; then, against the loft of afternoon clouds, they transcribe the rhetoric of flight. Ink drawings on a marbled parchment.

My mind grows still. Like water after all the ripples have played out, it reflects the world around it as it is. There is nothing I need to do to either create or hold on to this moment. In the presence of the cranes, I am a heartbeat only.

21

Shot Down

This moment has been aimed at me for nearly a week, like a tornado with something on its mind. Now that it is here, now that I am irrevocably broken down, car phone inoperable, arteries clogged, wings clipped, out in the middle of the Planet of the Potatoes, I accept my fate without protest. I sit in the wide doorway of the bus, bones hanging loose, a slight sun lightly glazing my arms and legs. In all directions, lumpy brown stubble. No houses. No cars passing. No thing moving, except for the cranes. They pull by me in dark chains, their wings stroking the cool air like oars. Wave after wave, rising and falling, like my breath. Like my spirits.

When I started out this morning, I was not worried; the bus would get fixed in either Alamosa or Monte Vista, and I would get back to Connecticut a couple of days later than I wished. No big deal. But as I lurched along through the two towns, rejected by one repair shop after another because no one worked on foreign cars, I began to feel trapped. Southern Colorado is shaped like a bowl—you have to climb up to get out of it. At that point, I was having trouble scaling Monte

Vista's speed bumps. At the last shop on the far edge of town, an empathetic mechanic made some calls for me, finally locating Peter, who lived twenty-six miles to the north in the potato fields. Peter said he would have a look. No guarantees.

Leaving the safety of town was probably foolish, but I couldn't conceive of abandoning my tiny home, my beautiful trip. And I had the car phone, or so I thought. Still it was daunting to put the bus in second gear, the last Tastee-Freez at my back, and lunge off into the empty space on the map. Several miles out, the oil buzzer started drilling my brain, and then the bus began to buck and weave like an exhausted bronco, as if that was all it had left to do. I kept moving, though, my right wheels on the far edge of the road. Several heart-dunking times the engine quit, but I was able to get it going again and grapple forward for another quarter of a mile or so. I knew I was spurring my old bus to its death, but I couldn't figure out what else to do.

A state police cruiser has just dropped out of the sky, deus ex machina style. My car phone, bought for this exact moment in time, couldn't even make it over the next potato field. While the policeman calls Peter for me, I inspect a melancholy figure sitting passively in the front seat of the cruiser. A Mexican farmworker, I guess, heavy mustache, wide-brimmed straw hat. He doesn't notice me at all; his eyes are locked on some vanished point beyond the horizon. Then I see his handcuffs and look away quickly, chastised somehow by his humiliation, as if I had further ridiculed him, peering at him that way.

The policeman tells me that Peter can't come for me because there is no one around to mind his shop, that he'd try to get hold of his daughter, but it could be a couple of hours or so before anyone shows up.

Fine, I think, as I return to the bus. I'll just sit in the sun and watch the cranes until help comes. I get out my binoculars, but they remain on my lap. Like the captive in the police car, my mind is riveted to something else, something that hasn't happened yet. A long time passes. I get back in the driver's seat and sit there squinting at the empty road. The cranes pass over me like ghosts; I have dismissed them, shunted them out of my mind.

A large Chevy Suburban has just roared up, cranked around, and backed up in front of me. A compact young woman wearing a heavy black-and-white-checked shirt jumps down, pulls a large chain out of the backseat, and approaches me. *This is my tow?* Nodding briefly toward me, she ducks under my front bumper and clips the chain. Then, without a backward glance, she snaps the chain to her car, gets in, and guns her engine. I quickly pop the hand brake and slam the bus into neutral just as she bolts off. I feel totally out of control, like a water-skier being towed by Madame Evel Knievel on her way to a flying leap. There are about fifteen terrifying feet of chain between us. What if she puts on the brakes? Bam, that's what.

"Focus, Anne. Focus!" I mutter to myself over and over. Pumping myself with the wheel, knuckles hard as rocks, my right foot poised over the brake pedal, I mirror her every move, knowing that at some point she has got to make a ninety-degree turn. She has forgotten about me, never checks her rearview mirror, never signals. And her speed never wavers, sixty miles an hour on the nose. Suddenly, without slowing down at all, her left blinker begins to pulse. Brake lights flash. I jam on mine, the chain goes slack, she starts the turn. Wham. The chain snaps tight, yanks me to the left. I wheel as fast as I can, closing in on her, brakes pumping, dirt whirling, gravel exploding, then silence. I am sitting two feet away from her bumper, my body crazy with adrenaline.

She gets out of the truck, no eye contact, unhooks the chain, and disappears into the shop. I wait there, humped in the driver's seat, dealing with the jumbo heart slamming away in my chest. A long time passes before an older man who looks a lot like the young woman appears.

"Gotta eat now," he says as he walks right by me. "I'll be back in an hour."

Well, at least I still have my home for another hour, I say to myself, as I take out the stove, set it down on the packed clay of the parking area, and brew up a cup of coffee. The house where Peter and his daughter eat their lunch sits near the repair shop. These two structures along with the silo across the way make up the nearest thing to a settlement in this part of Colorado. I sit on the ground in my Crazy Creek chair, sipping the warm sweet liquid, jotting notes on a legal pad, and watching potatoes bump down a chute into waiting trucks. They stack up higher and higher into impossible pyramids until, one potato too many, they all start rolling down the sides.

A vintage hotel on the main street of Monte Vista. Peter's daughter was kind to drive me all the way back here. She never really spoke to me though, not even when we got hit by a landslide of potatoes cascading off the truck in front of us. Bump bump bump bump they went, all over the hood of the Chevy. I guess people out here must get hit by potatoes all the time. Peter doesn't know what's wrong with the bus. He told me it's hard to get parts out there where he lives and that I should call him tomorrow afternoon.

I am sitting on the bed in my tiny room, my laptop before

me. The black rectangle of a window shows me how I look. I don't like what I see. Is this because I have been bickering with David on the phone? He said, "Just leave it there. Fly home." As if my journey were already over. I'm too bummed to write anymore tonight.

The window of my motel room in Pueblo, Colorado, frames a tangle of interstate feeders. Yesterday, a tow truck from Alamosa dragged the bus 180 miles up and over the mountains. I now wait to hear if the VW mechanics have been able to locate a rebuilt catalytic converter. When I was watching out for Peter's daughter, I felt myself freeze up like the bus. Sitting there nailed to the driver's seat, my body straining forward, all I was capable of was horizon patrol. My migration had stopped, and even though the cranes were still floating by, etching their story into the wide Colorado sky, I no longer had the energy or the desire to decipher it.

I am amazed how quickly I got sucked up by the future. In spite of all that I have learned on this journey, one minute I was there, fully present in my life, and then I was out of there, leaving just enough behind to go through the motions and take care of things. What frightens me is that this is how we live most of the time. Planning ahead. Waiting for things to happen. Judging from my present state of mind, it is not even half a life.

In the neglected parking lot of an abandoned motel next door to my motel, two spectacular western magpies search through clumps of grasses where sunflowers have taken root. Their yellow blossoms wag and bounce in a crisp wind blowing down from the north. A large quail has just popped out from under an abandoned car. Behind it comes a quail parade, one, two, three, four, five, six, seven. Quail-stepping, they march across the ragged no-man's-land, holding proper file except for the last runty one, who can't seem to get in step. When they reach the grassy patches around the Dumpster, they break ranks and begin to peck around. I locate my binoculars, steady my elbows on the windowsill, and jump into the scene. A dark form suddenly nudges into my peripheral vision. Black-and-white fur, red bell collar. The cat from the lobby of my motel, belly to the ground, slides slowly into a wall of weeds near the Dumpster. Measuring carefully, he coils his body up tight and springs with amazing force.

The knot of quails simply dilates, opening up a perfect bull's-eye for the cat to land in. Then the tiny regiment calmly comes to attention, strikes up the band, and struts over to the old motel, where it disappears under a crumbling porch. The cat skulks after them, pantherlike, barely parting the grass. Clearly, this has happened before.

22

Homing

I do not have visions, but there are images that appear to me without my bidding. They exist in the way that truths exist, solitary presences, waiting to be discovered.

As I head straight for Connecticut on I-80, the Platte River glinting like mica in this bright Nebraska afternoon, I sense the presence of strong cranes powering their huge dark wings overhead, even though it was days ago that they crossed over this river. Their existence is not a question, it is a force. Like them, I am homing. A sweet rushing rises like sound inside of me as I fit myself into their slipstream.

A few weeks before he died so suddenly last May, Peter Holroyd, a fearless Episcopal priest, mystic, and friend, took pity on me as we sat side by side in David's church. It was Morning Prayer, a service I do not look forward to.

"I don't like this service either," he had murmured into my ear as we wobbled on our knees during the longest stretch. Head still bowed, he'd given me a cryptic smile and then continued his prayers. That he had caught me stumbling on words, omitting phrases, trying to be a good minister's wife and hold on to my own dignity at the same time, was embarrassing, but it was also a blessing.

At that time, Peter, a deeply committed environmentalist, was leading a five-week program at David's church entitled "Spirit and Nature." During those weeks, his last on earth, he pointed me toward a spiritual life that was not bound by the language of traditional religious liturgy. Spirituality, according to Peter, was the awareness of one's place in the cosmos. Nothing more. Nothing less.

I am surprised by the fact that I keep thinking there's something more that I am supposed to be doing. That there are acts required. What is it, I find myself asking, that I need to do to experience the world as sacred?

Right now, right here in Nebraska, the sacred spreads out around me like an answer with no question attached to it. I remember feeling this kind of freedom a few years ago, after I chanced upon a monk dancing in the moonlight at Tengbouche Monastery, high up in the Everest region of Nepal. That night the peaks were blue-white fires.

On our way to Everest Base Camp, we had set up camp for the night in the grounds of the monastery. Just as it was growing dark, I heard the clamoring of cymbals and the ungodly moan of a horn coming from the central building of the sprawling complex. Threading my way through shadowy passages, I reached a wide central courtyard just as the last light slid off the monastery walls. At the top of some wooden steps, a huge navy blue-and-white canvas curtain covered the entrance to the main shrine room. Removing my shoes, I slipped into the darkness surrounding the candlelit rows of monks.

The *tulku* (reincarnated lama), revered by all highland Buddhists, was chanting in a deep voice as he tossed handfuls of rice up into the air. Every now and then, all the monks would fling rice up into the light of the butter lamps, an act that triggered a splintering crash of cymbals, the braying of horns, and the high trill of handbells. It was very very cold in the huge room, but I was totally mesmerized by the churn of the low voices, the jarring dissonance of the instruments. The ritual moved forward in waves, like a flying sea, exploding again and again on the shore. "Purification," I said to myself. "They are purifying the cosmos." This made sense. In a couple of days, when the moon was full, the monks of Tengbouche would perform their annual ritual dance, called *Mani Rimdu*. I had read that when the monks put on their costumes and begin to dance the ancient patterns, they actually become the gods and demons they portray.

A hand on my arm snapped me back into the world. "Dinner, memsahib!" I turned to find Ang Nima, one of our sherpas, crouched beside me. "You forgot dinner," he chided.

"I'm coming soon," I replied. "Please save some chapati and rice for me. That's all I want."

Once the spell was broken, I became acutely aware of my nearly frozen feet. I got up quietly and crept, head low, back hunched, toward my shoes at the rear entrance. When I stepped out from behind the huge blue-and-white canvas curtain, the moonlight nearly blinded me. The granite slabs in the courtyard below glowed softly, like the interior of a shell. As I started down the stairway, a dark figure wheeled briskly out of the shadows to my right. I froze in midstep. Like a windup toy, the figure spun one way, stopped dead, and spun the other way, rigidly, perfectly, tracing a dark path of curls across the silent moonscape. Each time he rotated toward the moon, I was stunned again by his face, by the rapture on it. I realized then that this was not a monk, dancing in the moonlight. It was the god. And I knew this without question or apology.

*   *   *

My mother is not a blue heron. A wild bird does not live inside of me. There are no bears in the woods or dragons in the night sea. And I cannot fly. These words are correct. But I do not think that they are true.

I have come to believe that these kinds of images are windows that open up onto all that has passed and all that is to come. They are the means by which I can connect myself with everything that is not myself. During the past few weeks, the birds winging overhead created an opening through which I have migrated out into the stars. These windows will change again and again in my lifetime, but the nature of their truths will always be the same.

In two more days, I'll be home. I think about the "home bed," its four graceful posters, its damask sheets and goose-down comforter. David's long body in the silver light. If a manx shearwater can get back to its tiny burrow after flying across the Atlantic Ocean, I can surely find my way back to my six-by-five-foot nest in the cosmos. The sooner the better.

23

The Black Swan

The black swan is very much in my thoughts this morning as the world beyond the French doors of our bedroom tightens with the cold. The pond is black, shining in the sun like a wet stone. It surprises me that I think about the swan so often, and that I miss her the way I do.

I first saw her on a midsummer night four months ago, just before I left on my trip in the blue bus. David and I had decided to stretch out the August twilight by taking a walk on Avon Mountain. We set out on one of the paths that thread through the watershed area just after sunset, in the glowing time between the colors and the dark. As we wandered through the woods and open meadows, fireflies resolved one by one, imitating the first stars materializing above our heads. By the time we turned down the last stretch of dike, the light was green and deep.

When I first saw her, gliding out of the inky shadows along the back edge of the pond, I didn't know what I was looking at. Grabbing David's arm, I pointed into the darkness. "What is that? I must be having a hallucination."

"Good lord," he responded in a hushed voice. "I don't know."

The silhouette paused for a moment, black on gray, the substance of dream. "It looks like a black swan," I ventured.

"I think you're right," David said, exhaling at last, "but I don't understand it."

We began creeping down the side of the dike, hunching up our bodies lest we disturb the fragile image teetering on the lip of reality before us. She slid out into the center of the small pond, as if to prove herself. She was small and perfect, her beauty staggering.

The light of day brought forward quite a different beginning to this story. Unable to find black swans in any of my bird books, I phoned the naturalist at our local nature center, as I have so many times before.

"Jay, is there such a thing as a black swan or have I lost my mind?"

"Yes, there is. In Australia," he answered in his impeccably matter-of-fact voice, "and I know where you saw one."

This didn't surprise me. Jay always knows these things. "I put it there. I think it was early in July." He went on to tell me about coming upon a traffic jam on Avon Mountain while he was on his way to a meeting in Rhode Island. "There, right in the middle of the four-lane highway, were two completely disoriented black swans, straggling back and forth on the asphalt, spooked by the stopped cars and by the policeman who was trying to shoo them off the road. So I just grabbed them, stuck one under each arm, and stashed them in the nearest pond. I figured I could deal with them later."

"Didn't they try to attack you?" I asked. I had heard that swans can be pretty nasty and that they are very strong.

"No, they were too freaked out. It was like scooping up a couple of puppies. When I got back from Rhode Island, I spent three or four days calling exotic bird suppliers, trying to track down the owners. It turned out that the swans had wandered away from a private pond about a mile away. I called the owners and told them exactly where they could find them. I knew the birds were not going anywhere soon because they were so traumatized by their outing, and they couldn't fly anywhere because they were pinioned."

The end of Jay's account was disheartening. After he'd waited a couple of weeks, he had gone back to the pond to see if the owners had retrieved the birds. He found only one swan. The other, he supposed, had become a meal for coyotes. He called the owners again to see what their intentions were. They told him they had already bought another pair and they had no plans for the marooned swan. He added, without editorializing, "I heard the new pair were picked off by coyotes a couple of weeks later."

As the summer deepened, it became clear the swan was on her own. I would often stop to see her on my way home from work. There, sitting on the side of the dike, I would escape through the lenses of my binoculars to where she was bathing and preening, shaking and refolding her wings, tugging at lush tubers growing in the soft dark muck. She became a kind of secret I carried around in my psyche, a vision that could open up a very ordinary afternoon like a window. Just the thought of her gave me access to a more sacred, more perfect world.

There was never any question about her being there. Jay had explained the practice of pinioning to me, an operation that renders birds permanently flightless and therefore defenseless, developed solely to keep waterfowl on their owner's property. The procedure involves removing the "hand," the outer part of the wing, including both the flight feathers and the bones that bear them. This was not new to

me. I had grown up near a city park where most of the waterfowl were clipped. Still, the first time I saw the swan's brutal-
ized stump, I felt sick. It was not just the ugliness but the loss
of sky, the grounding.

It must have been about the time the first geese passed
over our house in September that I realized the full implica-
tions of this surgery. The black swan could not migrate.
Sometime during the coming months, the pond would freeze
over. Her source of food would be sealed up, and the coyotes
would be waiting.

On my trip in the blue bus, I tried not to think about her
peril, but it was hard not to while witnessing the reality of
migration on such a massive scale. Shortly after my return,
the role I was to play in her story became clear.

David and I had driven down to Rhode Island to close up
the family cottage for the winter. Once again I went for a run
along my favorite shore road. As I ran by the spot where I had
first begun to think about migration two months before, I
saw that the ambers had gone on to browns, the reds to rus-
sets. The birds of summer had gone on too, replaced now by
speckled loons from the north, their throats whitening with
the shortening days. I sensed the light tap of a page turning. A
fresh one unfolded before me. At that moment a powerful
sensation of accord, still and full as the incoming tide, filled
my body. For one wonderful moment I saw the design. I
understood that the more perfectly we move within it, the
more perfectly we will live out our lives here, that even though
the complexity of our lives makes it difficult to decipher order
and purpose, our bodies still hold that knowledge. Even
though the lost language is muted, we can still hear it, and we
can still respond to it.

On the way home that evening, we pulled into the little
parking spot by the dike and hiked in to visit the swan. Watch-

ing her drift innocently in the autumn twilight, I made up my mind: somehow I was going to save her.

Early the next morning I drove over to the nature center. Jay was out in back in one of the large cages, filling the water bowls of two injured bald eagles now in residence there.

"Jay, we've got to catch the black swan. Soon!" I said urgently, forgetting to say hello.

"No biggie," he answered. He closed the pen door and unlatched a smaller one. "Don't move too fast or you'll spook the owl." He turned to me. "Swans are pretty slow."

Jay's no-frills demeanor reflects his artistry with wild creatures. Watching him move in and out of the pens of wounded and sick birds, I noted the economy of his actions, the way he pared each motion down to minimize his intrusion into their world.

"I need your help," I said. "I don't know how to catch a swan."

"Okay," he said, his dark brown eyes suddenly animated. "Here's what you have to do. You get her to come out of the pond, say about twenty feet or so. I'll get between her and the water, and then I'll grab her." He looked at my puzzled expression and then smiled wryly. "The answer to your question is Wonder Bread. It's cheap and it's soft."

"Is it good for her?" I asked. I felt I was getting in way over my head.

He looked at me steadily for a moment, making sure I was listening carefully. "That's not the point. The point is we're going to try to save her. And we don't have much time."

As I walked toward the parking lot, he called after me, "How do you know it's a her?"

I turned back, ignoring the bemused tilt of his head. "I just know. Seeya."

An hour later, I realized that our plan, simple as it sounded, was going to be very difficult to accomplish. The black swan had changed a good deal since the day Jay had snatched her off the highway. During the months she had been alone she had turned feral, and she no longer associated humans with feeding or safety. What did she care about Wonder Bread? As far as she knew, there was food enough in the dark water to satisfy her needs.

I visited her at least once a day, often twice. I would stand by the pond, talking to her and throwing bits of bread into the water, while she, without a backward glance, would sail away into the cattails on the far side, leaving me talking to myself.

One day, feeling utterly stumped, I decided to invade her territory. I circled the pond, rolled up my jeans, double knotted my running shoes, and slogged into the cattails. I soon found myself wallowing up to my knees in the muck. When the glop reached the middle of my thighs, I became nervous, remembering the time I helped rescue a fisherman who got stuck in a similar pond in Canton. By the time we got him uncorked, he had sunk up to his armpits and was pretty scared.

Driving home in my clammy clothes, I was close to giving up. The task seemed impossible, and the days were getting colder and colder. My frustration was heightened by the fact that Jay had called the night before to find out how things were progressing and to tell me that he had found a perfect home for her in a private sanctuary that was not only beautiful and safe but also the home of a male black swan who needed a partner.

Mandy was with me the day the mallards arrived. Home for the weekend, she had quickly offered to help when she sensed the ebb of my optimism. It was a glorious November day. A bold sun was flashing on the water and a fresh wind cutting in from the west. Having failed to attract the swan, we were sitting by the pond, enjoying the sun. Mandy had chosen that moment to tell me she was quitting her terrific job in advertising to become a writer. I remember flopping back into the grass, arms raised to the gods, my visions of her beautiful benefits winging toward the horizon. "I must be the worst mother in history," I wailed.

"No you're not," she said coyly, her huge eyes bounding with mirth.

You could go water-skiing in those eyes, I thought, ride dolphins. "Why not?" I implored. "None of my kids want to be normal. What kind of mother has kids that don't want to be normal?"

"The kind that has to save the goose," she answered, altogether pleased with herself.

"She's not a goose," I asserted petulantly.

Just then seven ducks came in low, surfing expertly right up to the swan, who was as usual lurking as far away from me as she could get. As soon as the ducks saw that we were offering Wonder Bread, they steamed right for us and began feeding eagerly just a few feet offshore. The black swan hung back for only a moment. Then, warily, she approached, stopping every few feet, turning as if to retreat, and turning again. When she was about fifteen feet away, I landed a small ball of the soft bread right in front of her. She poked at it, swallowed it, made a sweet little honk, and then moved forward to feed with the others. Mandy and I gaped at each other. It had been so easy! Then we hugged each other hard, thumping and hooting with relief.

Within days the swan was coming ashore for her bread. Usually, when I arrived, the pond would be blank, staring at me like an eye. Suppressing my panic, I would begin calling to her. She would come gliding out of the reeds, only her shadow disturbing the water, as if she were emerging from my consciousness. Then she would head straight for me. Every day I lured her a few feet farther from the safety of the pond. The mallards, who had been joined by one black duck, grew tamer as well.

I developed a swanly sort of voice, one I found rather embarrassing when caught at it by passing hikers or mountain bikers. She spoke to me too, in wistful little honks, and each day when I would reluctantly turn away and start back up the slope of the dike, she would protest with a high, sad bleat.

During the nights, when I would lie awake watching the cold stars swing through the high windows of our bedroom, images of two different swans would alternate in my thoughts. Sliding on the pale blue-gray surfaces of the water, the black swan manifested a dark grace. Ultimate, holy; she took my breath away every time. On the other hand, whenever she heaved herself ashore and began waddling toward me in her drunken-sailor roll, eyeballing me first with her left eye, then with her right, she became my funny, cranky friend. I loved the way she shamelessly relished her bread balls, the way she insisted on taking the bigger pieces of bread back to the edge to dunk, the way she tried to trick me into feeding her in the water by feigning indifference and returning to the pond after I had lured her a few feet farther than she was comfortable with. Once there, she would cruise back and forth about five feet offshore, looking annoyed. I would begin packing up my things, an act that would bring her scrambling out of the pond, pleading softly. I always let her win the last round of this game, would let her lead me to the water, where I would send whole pieces of bread floating out for her to dismantle at her leisure.

The weather remained warm well into November. The

deception of Indian summer, coupled with my infatuation, had somewhat obscured the urgency of the task ahead. By mid-November, she was almost coming up to me. Every day I would back up a couple of feet, coaxing her farther from safety, creating a stage for the drama to come.

When the first cuff of ice grew out from the shore, I felt as if I'd been slapped in the face. I skipped balls of bread onto the glassy surface, pleading with her to try and break it with her weight. She just sailed back and forth in the center of the pond, impatiently waiting for me to do something about it. The ducks, always more adventurous, drew into a wedge formation and broke trail through the ice until it became too thick. Then they heaved themselves up onto it and careened toward me like crazed acrobats, making dramatic headfirst slides-for-life as they competed for the bread balls that were scatted around on the ice. The swan watched from afar. Aloof. Patient.

I decided to try to break a channel out to her. On the far side of the dike near the road, I found some large rocks. One armful at a time, I lugged them up and over the top, creating a small arsenal next to the reeds. Then I lobbed the first rock. It arced through the air gracefully and disappeared with a pathetic little thunk into the depths, leaving a hole the same size as the rock. After two minutes of polka-dotting, I was out of rocks and out of ideas.

That evening I called Jay. He asked a lot of questions about the weeks I had been working with her.

"Can you get her to come at least fifteen feet out of the pond every time?"

"Yes."

"How come she won't eat from your hand?"

"She's still pretty spooky. She gets confused when she comes too close."

"How close?"

"Two feet."

"Are you sure about all of this? You know we are only going to have one shot at this. Swans are not dumb."

We made a date to meet at the dike three days later. My sister, Nicki, and her partner, Sam, called to say they would like to be a part of the rescue attempt. Sam said he had located an old soccer net that he thought might be useful.

We met on the Friday before Thanksgiving. The day was hazy and mild, the bracelet of ice gone. Jay positioned himself near the edge of the pond, about twenty feet to the right of the spot where the swan usually came ashore. Sam stood with his net by the reeds to the left. Nicki was up on the side of the dike near me. The three of us had carefully practiced this positioning during the preceding days, and the swan had become used to having other people around.

She came right out, leading her gaggle of mallards and the one, now very tame, black duck. She shambled happily toward me, delighting in the trail of bread balls. As she contemplated each new find, she would look up at me, questioning, first with one eye, then with the other, "For me?"

She was feeding approximately twenty feet away from the edge of the pond and about two feet from me when Jay swooped down on her. Terrified, she bolted for the water, flapping her useless wings, honking, and spewing feathers. She flailed her way through the reeds at a remarkable speed.

Jay never even got close. She had outmaneuvered him, but she was pissed. There on the far side, she swam back and forth in an angry figure eight, like a jungle cat pacing in its cage. My eyes burned with tears. It was bad enough to have manipulated her trust, but now, having failed, I felt as if I had betrayed her.

That night it snowed several inches. I slept poorly, haunted by an image of the swan gliding around in the darkness with a wedge of snow on her back. The next morning I climbed back over the dike alone, ready to start all over again. I didn't have much hope, but I called out to her as usual. To my amazement, she swam right for me, piped her welcoming notes, and came ashore. I was ecstatic. Obviously she did not associate me with Jay's attack. She fed for a long time.

I knew I had to get her reeled in very tight before we tried again. Crouching as usual, I dropped some bread a few inches from my right toe. She protested, weaving and hissing. I waited her out, holding absolutely still, diverting my gaze as if indifferent. Eventually she located a "safe" tunnel below the line of my gaze and, believing she had tricked me, wormed her way under my outstretched arm and nabbed the coveted bread ball. The snow was melting quickly under a bright sun and my spirits soared. I called Jay to make another date while the weather was still fine.

"Why didn't you just grab her?" he asked after I gave him my update.

I had wondered about this myself. "Because I was afraid that if I missed I wouldn't get another chance," I said. But I knew this was only part of the truth. The other part had to do with betrayal.

The second grab took place at the end of the period of fair weather. We totally blew it, reenacting the previous scenario with appalling precision. This time there was no question about the effects of our bungling.

The swam retreated to the far side of the pond, snapping her head back and forth as she swam in a tight circle. I stayed a long time, talking to her, feeding the ducks, who readily forgave me even though they too had been terrorized. After an hour, I gathered a few of the black feathers that were caught in the rushes by the water, and turned toward the road. I was deeply discouraged. I missed the soft pleas that usually followed me up the dike.

That evening just as we were sitting down to dinner, Jay phoned. In a somber voice, he told me that he had been trying to contact the state fish and game people to see if they would be willing to try to catch her with one of their spring-loaded nets. We both knew these tricky devices often maimed and sometimes killed birds, but we were out of options and out of time. Jay finished his report with a warning. "The only problem is their offices are closed until after the Thanksgiving holiday, and that may be too late."

During the night I dreamed I flew again. It happened this way: I was on my way to school with a group of faceless friends. We were in high spirits, darting and sprinting down the evenly spaced squares of sidewalk pavement. Feeling strong, I began to lope out in front of the rest. As the stroke of my stride deepened, giddiness fluttered through my body like a trapped bird. I vaulted over one of the paving stones, clearing it easily. I leapt again. This time I floated for three or four squares. Suddenly I remembered all the other dreams, remembered that I know how to do this, and I powered up, took a tremendous leap, and sailed up into the cool air above the deep green clouds of leaves. Wild with energy, I circled over Avon Mountain, shouting down to the others, "You can do it. Just start bounding!"

I awoke from this dream and turned over on my side to watch the winter light brim up along the horizon. I was savoring the exhilaration of my night flight when suddenly I remembered the swan, saw her stump wagging grotesquely as she raced for the safety of the pond. *God,* I thought, *I flew right over her in my dream. She was the one I was calling down to.*

Thanksgiving was bitterly cold. The pond in front of our house closed up. Over the damask and the silver, the turkey and the pies, Sam and Nicki and David recounted the story of the black swan to our other guests. The story appeared to be gaining a mythic solidity, as if the terrible conclusion and its moral were already written. The weather forecasters were talking about an arctic freeze over the next three or four days. In spite of the fact that we were out of ideas, we made a plan to meet at the dike the next morning.

While the pond is hidden from the road by the dike, it is visible from the top of the mountain. As I came over the crest, my spirits sagged. The pond was steel gray, and only a small dark pupil of water remained open near the mouth of the brook on the far side. In it, still as a statue, floated the black swan.

When I pulled into the small parking area, I was surprised to see three bundled figures rocking and stomping their feet beside Sam's bus. To my great surprise, one of them was my nephew Scottie, an ornithologist who specializes in seabirds. On his infrequent visits home from far and wild places, he has mesmerized me with stories of encounters with the albatrosses he befriended on Tern Island in the middle of the Pacific Ocean. I had watched a video of him holding them in his arms and scratching their heads. "Albatrosses love to be petted," he'd explained casually.

"Scottie will know what to do," I whispered as I shut down the engine. "Please," I implored.

Once we tested the thickness of the ice, we agreed there wasn't much we could do. Scottie suggested that he and I go over to the far side, get as near as we could to the open spot, and try to lure her onto the ice. He gave me a mysterious smile. "I don't mind getting a little wet," he said.

The swan was so excited to see me that she did not seem to mind the down-padded figure crouching beside me in a tangle of brambles and brush. Even so, we could not get her to climb up on the ice and feed nearer the shore. Discouraged, I

threw all the rest of the bread to her, said good-bye, and tried
to ignore her calls as we walked back to our cars.

Nicki and Sam were pacing anxiously as we approached
the pullout. They had obviously been plotting.

"We've been talking this over," Sam began, "and we think
we can get her with a canoe."

"She will just take off into the cattails," I replied. "It won't
work. She's too fast. We'll drive her right into the mouths of
the coyotes."

"Wait a minute," Scottie interrupted. "It could work. Most
birds can't see very well at night. You can freeze them with a
spotlight and just scoop them up. I've done it lots of times."

We all looked at one another, big grins spreading, our eyes
sparking back and forth.

Sam took charge. "It gets dark by five. We'll bring the
canoe. You bring your wire dog crate, Anne—be sure to pad
it—and a spotlight and some flashlights. I'll bring the soccer
net."

After getting my equipment together, I spent the rest of
the afternoon putting Thanksgiving away. Occasionally, passing the coat rack by the front door, I would catch a glimpse of
my red expedition-weight parka, my Gore-Tex pants, and my
brand-new Wellingtons, three sizes too big, standing at attention, and my heart would pick up speed. "This is really crazy,"
I would mutter. "It can't work."

At five o'clock it was pitch-dark and terribly cold, with a
light skim of clouds revealing and then erasing a graceful
young moon. We unloaded the canoe off the top of Sam's VW
bus. Just a few yards away, home-bound cars hustled up the
mountain, unaware of the drama that was unfolding right
beside them.

Scottie gave us instructions. "Anne, you go locate her
while we carry the canoe over the dike." Frigid air stunning my

lungs, I set off down the dike toward the marshy area around the feeder stream. My footfall sounded absurdly loud as I crunched through the icy grasses. As I rounded the far side, I realized that the clouds were reflecting the pink lights of Hartford, just enough to create the faintest of twilights. I turned off my flashlight, and when my eyes became accustomed to the dark, I saw her silhouette clearly, a seamless figure floating in a pool not much larger than herself, in utter silence, backlit by the eerie dusk of the city. Yet again, her beauty astounded me; sharp tears blurred my sight. I felt I was seeing her for the last time.

The plan was that David and I, wearing high boots, would place ourselves fifty yards apart in the cattail marsh on the far side. Our job was to charge her and scare her back out onto the ice if she tried to flee in our direction. Scottie, the catcher, was to kneel in the bow of the canoe. Nicki, in the middle, was to hold the spotlight on the swan, and Sam, in the rear, had the job of propelling the canoe through the already solid ice.

David and I worked our way into the tall reeds, trying not to alarm the swan as we broke through the ice into knee-deep water. My oversized boots made it hard to compete with the suck of the mud as I slogged along. When I reached my designated spot, I felt deeply alone, isolated by an almost unbearable powerlessness. Up until this point, I had orchestrated the rescue with maternal care, my relationship with the swan forming the basis of all plans to save her. This relationship did not matter anymore, other than the fact that it had brought us to this moment. Now my only option was this surreal nighttime mission.

Suddenly a massive crash fractured the stillness. The canoe started lumbering in our direction like some terrible monster, shattering the ice in rhythmic explosions, filling the night with a convulsive violence. The swan reared up, wheeled in panic, and started flapping toward us. I screamed and tried to run toward her, but the muck was grabbing at my boots like a nightmare, the icy water sliding in. I could hear myself crying out, "Oh no. Oh no. Oh my God, no," as the crashing grew louder and louder. Abruptly the spotlight cut the darkness. I saw the swan, up on the ice, her wings flailing in pure terror. I saw Sam's silhouette: his arms, back, and shoulders plunging in herculean strokes as he willed a path through the thick ice. The canoe was now lunging like a whale, sending up huge broken sheets of ice. The noise was deafening. Then it stopped, and there was only a rigid silence.

"It's over," Nicki said softly, barely raising her voice. "We've got her."

Staggering out of the marsh in disbelief and shock, I saw the canoe retracing its way through the open path of water. In the bow, Scottie knelt, his left arm wrapped around the swan, holding her wings tightly against his body. His right hand, on the swan's neck, held her head pointed forward. When the boat reached the shore, he leapt out gracefully and, pressing the swan against his body, disappeared into darkness. The rest of us began lugging the canoe up the dike. At one point I looked back toward the pond and was able to identify Scottie's motionless form, crouching by the water, holding her tight.

That night, as I lay in bed, images from the incredible evening wove in and out of my dreaming mind. My arms could still feel the exact weight of the swan's body, her warmth, as I lifted her from the wire crate and carried her to the large holding pen in back of the nature center. And then, a bit later at Nicki and Sam's house, the crazy sense of joy and release that made us create goofy hats and turbans and decorate them with plastic and papier-mâché birds, made us set a place at the dinner table for Nicki's five-foot-tall inflated penguin, made us all laugh and laugh until our faces were wet, at each others' hats, at the damned penguin, at the wonder of it all.

Somewhere toward dawn, I realized that although this year's migration was over, for me, another one had already begun. In my mind I saw a long procession of people moving forward slowly. All the people of my life: the loved, the lost, the long gone. I saw myself among them, moving forward easily, as if there were all the time in the world. It came to me that we are all of us black swans: transplanted, pinioned, marooned in lands far, far away from the place of our first simple flocking, where time is articulated by the shadow of a wing, where poetry is born in mute and holy splendor. But the miracle is that we can still remember it at times, can still re-create it, at times, even if it is just for a moment.

I saw the swan one more time, about a year after we caught her. I can't say why I waited so long to visit her. She lives in paradise—there is no other word for the huge pond filled with exotic waterfowl, surrounded by nesting houses, natural vegetation, woods, and fences to keep predators out. "There are four black swans," Kem Appell, founder of the Connecticut Waterfowl Trust, told me as he let me into the enclosure. "They do everything together. Even sit on each other's eggs."

"Has she laid any?" I asked hopefully.

"Several, but no fertile ones yet," he answered. "Sometimes it takes a while."

Just then a black swan swaggered out of one of the large nesting houses, followed by three others. I recognized mine immediately, third in line. As they moved closer, I knelt down by the edge of the pond and began talking to her. The first two entered the water without pausing, but my swan stopped on the brink, and her partner halted right behind her. She rolled her head back and forth a few times, as if she was trying to place the sound of my voice. I could tell she was feeling conflicted. The couple in the water were bleating loudly. Her mate was poised behind her, waiting patiently. She hovered in abeyance for almost a minute, weaving her head slowly like a cobra, and then she slid out of my life forever, shielded by a swirl of flightless wings.

Autumn came, and I did not have to go away. To be sure, I felt the old restlessness, the longing, but this time it took the shape of a vibrant readiness, an unshakable certainty that something miraculous was on the brink of happening. And so it did. Day after day after day.

Throughout September and October the hawks passed through Connecticut in massive waves. The broad-wings were the first to arrive, riding the tailwinds of a powerful cold front. Nicki and I were waiting for them that chilly morning, flat on our backs in a hilltop meadow near her house, puffed up in down parkas, binos clamped tightly to our faces. For a very long time the sky was empty, and the only passersby were carloads of people on their way to work. We got pretty silly— the way sisters can—lying there like Pillsbury Doughboys, four little sneakers pointed skyward. Every time a car slowed down to check us out, Nicki would wail, "Why oh why must we humiliate ourselves like this?" Then we would guffaw until our tears ran into our wool hats.

The surprising thing was that the broad-wings did show up that day. As soon as it warmed up, they burst out of the green hills like feathers from a pillow, swirling upward in cyclonic towers until they hit the winds aloft and streamed away to the south. Twenty-five thousand of them did that, right before our eyes—as we learned when we called the nature center later in the day.

Before I left on my journey in the blue bus, I'd felt I had few choices left. The script of my future appeared to be as immutable as the one of my past. All that has changed. My days are filled with choices. Many of them have names: David, Anee, Mandy, the smudge of a galaxy in the eye of my telescope, a walk at nightfall, the silence of my meditation room, the skirling of blue jays when I wake at dawn. I now know, in some irreversible way, that these are thresholds, openings in the wall of the knee-jerk reality that most often passes for the real thing. It was the black swan who convinced me that the world as it presents itself is, at best, only partially revealed, that the truly extraordinary is always quickening on the far side of the ordinary.

As for the ghosts. They will, I suppose, always be out there, nosing around for a chink in the flow of my thoughts. After all, they are my ghosts: the clink of ice in a cocktail glass coming from the kitchen at eight in the morning, the deep chill of loneliness as it passes through the wall of a vacant afternoon, the scorch marks of my first marriage, the sound of children's laughter at the top of the stairs, my father's voice rising above the whack and slap of luffing sails. During my five weeks of solitude in the blue bus, I had to reckon with them all, to recognize, acknowledge, and release them, one by one by one, so that I could enter once again the seamless, mercurial, dazzling flux that is the present—and all we will ever really know of the future.

Some things, however, will never change. Once you've had a taste of dead reckoning, you never forget it. How it feels to be headed outbound, the past falling away, the future still to be created. Sometimes the urge to take off will flare up unexpectedly, as it did a few days ago. I do not know what brought it on; maybe it was the ice breaking up in our pond or maybe it was just the wild bird inside me flexing its wings. David and I were driving back from Hartford when I finally summoned up enough nerve to tell him I had been "thinking a lot about the blank spaces on the map up north of us, way up north."

He nodded slowly a couple of times but remained silent.

"Yesterday I got out the atlas and some old maps," I blundered on nervously. "I keep having this urge to drive north as far as the road goes, just to see where it stops."

I saw a smile playing at the corners of his mouth.

"What's so funny?" I asked defensively. "You know I've always wanted to go above the Arctic Circle."

"You are what's funny," he said, laughing that clear, clean laugh I love so much.

"That bad, huh?" I said, relieved because he was laughing . . . a good sign. Maybe I would be able to pull this one off.

"I keep hoping that someday they'll figure out that this is a certifiable condition and invent a pill to cure it," he said, shaking his head, "before you drive *me* crazy."

"That bad!" I reached over to touch his thigh. A tug of love, almost like tears, pulled at my eyes. *God, I'm lucky,* I said to myself.

"God, I'm lucky," I said to him, kissing the palm of his right hand.